英语版

Business
Communication in China

eriencing
Chinese

体验 汉语® **100** 句

商务类

编者　张　红

译者　陈会新

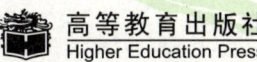

高等教育出版社
Higher Education Press

总 策 划　　刘　援

编　者　　张　红

译　者　　陈会新

英语审订　　Erin Harper

策划编辑　　徐群森

责任编辑　　李锡奎　金飞飞

封面设计　　彩奇风

版式设计　　高　瓦

插图选配　　陆　玲

责任校对　　金飞飞　李锡奎

责任绘图　　未来视界

责任印制　　宋克学

尊敬的读者：

您好！

欢迎您选用《体验汉语100句》系列丛书。

随着经济全球化的不断发展和中国国力的增强，世界范围内学习汉语的人数不断增加。为满足不同国度、不同领域、不同层次汉语学习者的需求，我社策划、研发了《体验汉语100句》系列丛书。该系列丛书包含生活类、留学类、商务类、旅游类、文化类、体育类、公务类、惯用表达类等诸方面，有针对性地帮助汉语学习者快捷地掌握相关领域中最常见、最实用的中文表达。

为满足各国汉语学习者的实际需要，每册书还配有英语、日语、韩语、法语、德语、俄语、西班牙语、泰语、印尼语等九个语言版本，今后还将开发更多语种的版本。

愿本书成为您步入汉语世界的向导，成为您了解中国的桥梁，也希望您提出意见和建议。欢迎您随时与我们联系。

高等教育出版社

前言

本书是《体验汉语100句》系列中的商务类。

《体验汉语100句》系列覆盖生活、留学、商务、旅游、文化、体育、公务、惯用表达等诸多方面，有针对性地帮助汉语学习者掌握相关领域中最常见、最实用的中文表达。

本书挑选商务工作中100个常用、地道的句子，按照10个类别学习，有助于汉语学习者解决商务工作中进行公司介绍、商务交流、财务、市场营销和贸易等具体活动的基本语言问题。

特 点

本书按照功能项目分类编排，包括人力资源、公司组织、商业交往、研发生产、市场营销、财务记录、证券市场、信息管理、金融服务和国际贸易10个项目。每个项目下选取的句子不仅实用，而且具有较强的生成性，适用范围较广，便于学习者今后深入的学习。

所有中文句子都标有拼音和英语译文，注释部分则直接用英文表达。每一句话都配有简单的替换练习，帮助您熟悉句型，扩大词汇量。

结 构

本书中每句话的学习包括常用句、对话、DIY和注释四个部分。

· 常用句

全书共收录100个句子，每个句子都用汉字、拼音和英语译文清楚地标明了句子的写法、读音和意义。

· 对话

对话内容均为在真实场景下使用的常用句，以帮助学习者理解句子的意思，并学会使用和应答。

· DIY

提供了几个替换练习，帮助读者进一步灵活应用每个句子。

· 注释

本栏目主要是为学习者介绍相关的商务背景知识，中国的商务环境、法律法规等，在帮助学习者学习语言的同时，加强其对中国商务环境与情况的了解。

编者

The *Experiencing Chinese 100* series contains phrases pertaining to living, studying, traveling, sports, popular Chinese idioms, cultural communication, official communication, business communication and many more areas of interest. This book is *Experiencing Chinese 100 (Business Communication in China)*.

In this book, we have chosen 100 representative sentences commonly used in business and divided them into ten categories. Studying these sentences will help learners of the Chinese language use basic language skills to settle questions arising from their business practice, including introduction of their companies, commercial exchanges, finance, marketing, trade and other activities.

Features

This book has been arranged according to the different functions of the sentences, including Human Resources, Company Organization, Business Communication, R&D and Production, Marketing, Financial Record, Securities Market, Information Management, Financial Service, and International Trade. Sentences chosen and arranged under the above ten categories are not only practical, but also widely applicable. They will contribute to learners' further exploration into the Chinese language in the future.

All the sentences are written in Chinese and *Pinyin* with English translations. Each sentence has a simple and easily studied substitution drill, helping to familiarize yourself with the sentence pattern and expand your vocabulary.

Structure

This book includes: Frequently Used Sentences (FUS), Conversation, DIY and Notes.

· FUS: There are a total of 100 sentences, each written in both Chinese characters and *Pinyin*, accompanied by an English translation.

· Conversation: Placing FUS in a realistic setting allows readers to better understand the meaning, usage and appropriate responses.

· DIY: After each sentence, DIY provides several exercises for readers to practice appropriate usage.

· Notes: This column is designed to briefly introduce background information on business, the commercial environment in China, and Chinese laws and regulations, so that readers also gain a better understanding of the above as they study the Chinese language.

目录 Contents

人力资源 2 Human Resources

公司组织 22 Company Organization

商业交往 42 Business Communication

研发生产 62 Research, Development and Production

市场营销 82 Marketing

财务记录 102 Financial Record

证券市场 122 Securities Market

信息管理 142 Information Management

金融服务 162 Financial Service

国际贸易 182 International Trade

附录 Appendix

中国的主要商业银行 202 Major Commercial Banks in China

中国常用机构网址 204 Commonly used websites of organizations in China

这是我的简历和求职信。

Zhè shì wǒ de jiǎnlì hé qiúzhíxìn.

This is my resume and application letter.

你带简历了吗？
Nǐ dài jiǎnlì le ma?

带了，这是我的简历和求职信。
Dài le, zhè shì wǒ de jiǎnlì hé qiúzhíxìn.

Have you brought your resume with you?
Yes, I have. This is my resume and application letter.

这是我的简历和＿＿＿＿＿。

zhè shì wǒ de jiǎnlì hé

证书
zhèngshū
certificate

推荐信
tuījiànxìn
recommendation letter

学位证
xuéwèizhèng
academic degree certificate

NOTES

Documents needed for a job applying include their resume, application letter, academic record, certificates that prove their competence in foreign languages and computer skills, certificates of honor, certificates of professional qualification and others.

我做过 5 年的市场营销。

Wǒ zuò guò wǔ nián de shìchǎng yíngxiāo.

I have worked in the marketing business for five years.

● 你有工作经验吗？
Nǐ yǒu gōngzuò jīngyàn ma?

● 有，我做过 5 年的市场营销。
Yǒu, wǒ zuò guò wǔ nián de shìchǎng yíngxiāo.

● Do you have any work experience?
● Yes, I have worked in the marketing business for five years.

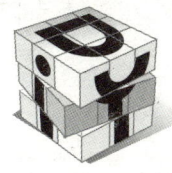

我 做 过 5 年 的 _____。
wǒ zuǒ guò wǔ nián de

人力资源
rénlì zīyuán

human resources

财务管理
cáiwù guǎnlǐ

finance management

软件开发
ruǎnjiàn kāifā

software development

NOTES

Recruitment advertisements in various media show that almost all enterprises have rather high requirements for applicants' work experience, which is a sharp contrast compared to many enterprises' sole demand for "Fluency in English" in previous years.

他从北京大学毕业，取得了硕士学位。

Tā cóng Běijīng Dàxué bìyè, qǔdé le shuòshì xuéwèi.

He graduated from Peking University with a Master's degree.

○ 他有什么学历？

Tā yǒu shénme xuélì?

● 他从北京大学毕业，取得

Tā cóng Běijīng Dàxué bìyè, qǔdé

了硕士学位。

le shuòshì xuéwèi.

○ What was the highest education he got?

● He graduated from Peking University with a Master's degree.

他从北京大学毕业，取得
tā cóng Běijīng Dàxué bìyè qǔdé

了_____学位。
le xuéwèi

学士
xuéshì

bachelor degree

博士
bóshì

doctoral degree

Statistics from China's National Bureau of Statistics show that in 2005, there were a total of 2273 regular and adult higher education institutions (HEI) in China, with the scale of HEI student enrollment and new student enrollment increasing continuously. In 2005, total enrollment in all HEIs in China exceeded 23 million, with the gross enrollment rate reaching 21%. Student enrollment for HEI graduate and undergraduate education were 364,800 and 504,460,000, respectively.

4

她的专业是饭店管理，今年又通过了·HSK 7级。
Tā de zhuānyè shì fàndiàn guǎnlǐ, jīnnián yòu tōngguò le HSK7 jí.

She majored in hotel management and she passed the HSK 7 this year.

● 珍妮的专业是什么？
Zhēnnī de zhuānyè shì shénme?

● 她的专业是饭店管理，今年
Tā de zhuānyè shì fàndiàn guǎnlǐ, jīnnián

又通过了 HSK7 级。
yòu tōngguò le HSK7 jí.

● What was Jane's major?
● She majored in hotel management, and she passed the HSK 7 this year.

她 的 专 业 是 ＿＿＿＿＿＿＿，
tā de zhuānyè shì

今 年 又 通 过 了 H S K 7 级 。
jīnnián yòu tōngguò le HSK7 jí

工业设计
gōngyè shèjì

industrial design

市场营销
shìchǎng yíngxiāo

marketing

国际贸易
guójì màoyì

international trade

NOTES

HSK (Hanyu Shuiping Kaoshi) is a standardized test at the state level established to assess test-takers' proficiency in the Chinese language. It consists of four levels: HSK Basic, HSK Elementary, HSK Intermediate and HSK Advanced. HSK is held regularly in China and overseas each year. HSK Certificates will be issued to those who have secured required scores. HSK Certificates are recognized by many companies.

她通过了笔试和面试，已经被一家公司录用了。

Tā tōngguò le bǐshì hé miànshì, yǐjīng bèi yì jiā gōngsī lùyòng le

She has passed the written examination and the interview, and is now employed by a company.

● 爱米找到工作了吗？

Àimǐ zhǎo dào gōngzuò le ma?

● 她通过了笔试和面试，

Tā tōngguò le bǐshì hé miànshì,

已经被一家公司录用了。

yǐjīng bèi yì jiā gōngsī lùyòng le.

● Has Amy found a job?

● She has passed the written examination and the interview, and is now employed by a company.

她通过了笔试和面试，已经
tā tōngguò le bǐshì hé miànshì yǐjīng

被＿＿＿＿＿＿录用了。
bèi lùyòng le

一家企业
yì jiā qǐyè

an enterprise

一所学校
yì suǒ xuéxiào

a school

这个部门
zhège bùmén

this department

NOTES

According to Chinese laws, when an employer is to employ a staff, the staff is not entitled to this employment unless he has concluded his labor contract with his previous employer; otherwise this employment would become an illegal one.

报纸上有你们公司的招聘广告。

Bàozhǐ shang yǒu nǐmen gōngsī de zhāopìn guǎnggào.

There are recruitment advertisements for your company in the newspaper.

● 你是怎么知道公司的招聘

Nǐ shì zěnme zhīdào gōngsī de zhāopìn

信息的？

xìnxī de?

● 报纸上有你们公司的招聘

Bàozhǐ shang yǒu nǐmen gōngsī de zhāopìn

广告。

guǎnggào.

● How did you learn about our company's recruitment information?

● There are recruitment advertisements for your company in the newspaper.

_____有你们公司的招聘
yǒu nǐmen gōngsī de zhāopìn

广告。
guǎnggào

网上
wǎng shang

on the internet

电视上
diànshì shang

on the TV

杂志上
zázhì shang

in magazines

NOTES

"Zhāopìn" is what companies and other employers do. For an individual, it is "yìngpìn". People can get recruitment information from media like newspapers, magazines, radio stations, websites and headhunting companies.

这个公司的福利好不好？

Zhège gōngsī de fúlì hǎobùhǎo?

How are the benefits at this company?

● 这个公司的福利好不好？

Zhège gōngsī de fúlì hǎobùhǎo?

● 听说他们的工资不高，

Tīngshuō tāmen de gōngzī bù gāo,

但福利不错。

dàn fúlì búcuò.

● How are the benefits at this company?

● It is said that employees enjoy good benefits, though their salaries are not so high.

这个公司的＿＿＿＿好不好？
zhège   gōngsī   de   hǎobùhǎo

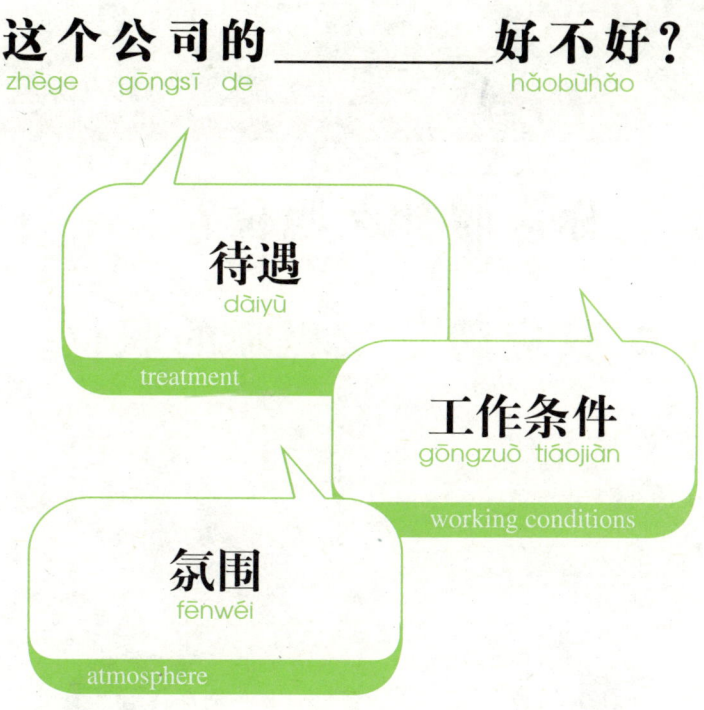

待遇
dàiyù

treatment

工作条件
gōngzuò tiáojiàn

working conditions

氛围
fēnwēi

atmosphere

A company's benefits usually include social insurance, medical insurance, housing loans, and so like.

15

我应聘总工程师的职位。

Wǒ yìngpìn zǒng gōngchéngshī de zhíwèi.

I am applying for the position of Chief Engineer.

● 你应聘什么职位？
Nǐ yìngpìn shénme zhíwèi?

● 我应聘总工程师的职位。
Wǒ yìngpìn zǒng gōngchéngshī de zhíwèi.

○ What position are you applying for?
● I am applying for the position of Chief Engineer.

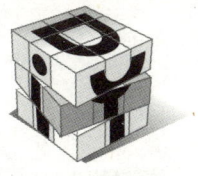

我 应 聘 ＿＿＿＿＿＿ 的 职 位 。
wǒ yìngpìn   de zhíwěi

研发经理
yánfā jīnglǐ

manager in research and development

秘书
mìshū

secretary

行政助理
xíngzhěng zhùlǐ

administrative assistant

NOTES

When people choose their vocations, they probably take into account the content, intensity, and environment of that certain job, as well as their income and welfare. Nowadays, people tend to think more about room and opportunity for their professional development. The number of people taking salary as top priority is now on the decline.

你参加过职业培训吗？

Nǐ cānjiā guò zhíyè péixùn ma?

Have you attended any professional training sessions?

● 你参加过**职业培训**吗？

　　Nǐ cānjiā guò zhíyè péixùn ma?

● 一年前参加过。

　　Yì nián qián cānjiā guò.

培训事业部

● Have you attended any professional training sessions?

● I attended one year ago.

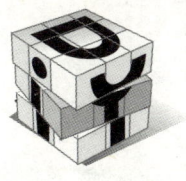

你参加过_____吗？
nǐ cānjiā guò   ma

招聘
zhāopìn

recruitment

面试
miànshì

interview

NOTES

There are two common professional trainings. One is "reemployment training", which is conducted to help those who have lost their jobs to learn certain cultural knowledge and technical skills to become qualified labors, so that they might get reemployed. The other is called "on-the-job training", which is conducted to help new employees of a company to understand the company's values and corporate culture, as well as to foster their teamwork spirit, so that this new recruit will adapt him/herself to new position.

19

公司决定提升王伟为营销总监。

Gōngsī juédìng tíshēng Wáng Wěi wéi yíngxiāo zǒngjiān.

The company has decided to promote Wang Wei to Chief Marketing Officer.

● 听说王伟最近干得不错。

Tīngshuō Wáng Wěi zuìjìn gàn de búcuò.

● 是啊，所以公司决定提升

Shì a, suǒyǐ gōngsī juédìng tíshēng

王伟为营销总监。

Wáng Wěi wéi yíngxiāo zǒngjiān.

● I heard that Wang Wei has been doing well recently.

● That's right. That is why the company has decided to promote Wang Wei to Chief Marketing Officer.

公司决定＿＿＿＿＿王伟为
gōngsī juédìng　　　　Wáng Wěi wéi
营销总监。
yíngxiāo zǒngjiān

任命
rènmìng

appoint

聘用
pìnyòng

engage

委派
wěipài

accredit

NOTES

Most basic and intermediate position vacancies in Chinese companies are filled according to an internal promotion policy, so as to build up cohesion within the company, encourage employees to make greater achievements, and allow those outstanding employees who have made greater contributions to the company a bigger stage to exert their competence.

李先生是公司的董事长。

Lǐ xiānsheng shì gōngsī de dǒngshìzhǎng.

Mr. Li is the chairman of the board of the company.

● 谁是公司的董事长？
Shuí shì gōngsī de dǒngshìzhǎng?

● 李先生是公司的董事长。
Lǐ xiānsheng shì gōngsī de dǒngshìzhǎng.

● Who is the chairman of the board of the company?
● Mr. Li is the chairman of the board of the company.

李先生是公司的 _____。
Lǐ xiānsheng shì gōngsī de

董事
dǒngshì

Director

总经理
zǒngjīnglǐ

General Manager

副总经理
fùzǒngjīnglǐ

Deputy General Manager

In order to improve the structure of corporate governance, many joint-stock companies are including more independent directors in the board. The main role of independent directors is to prevent the interests of middle and small stock holders from being harmed.

金女士负责公司的管理工作。

Jīn nǚshì fùzé gōngsī de guǎnlǐ gōngzuò.

Ms. Jin is responsible for the management of the company.

金女士负责什么工作？
Jīn nǚshì fùzé shénme gōngzuò?

金女士负责公司的管理
Jīn nǚshì fùzé gōngsī de guǎnlǐ

工作。
gōngzuò.

What is Ms. Jin responsible for?

Ms. Jin is responsible for the management of the company.

金女士负责公司的＿＿＿＿＿
jīn nǚshì fùzé gōngsī de
工作。
gōngzuò

财务
cáiwù

financing

销售
xiāoshòu

sales

公关
gōngguān

public relations

NOTES

Managers have changed the operational model of world commerce. They are the real leading players of the market economy, are creating more and more job opportunities, and are making more and more people rich.

这家上市公司的总经理非常能干。

Zhè jiā shàngshì gōngsī de zǒngjīnglǐ fēicháng nénggàn.

The General Manager of this listed company is really efficient.

- 这家上市公司的总经理
  Zhè jiā shàngshì gōngsī de zǒngjīnglǐ

  非常能干。
  fēicháng nénggàn.

- 怪不得公司经营得这么好。
  Guàibudé gōngsī jīngyíng de zhème hǎo.

- The General Manager of this listed company is really efficient.
- No wonder this company is doing so well.

这家上市公司的总经理
zhè jiā shàngshì gōngsī de zǒngjīnglǐ

非常＿＿＿＿＿＿＿。
fēicháng

有经验
yǒu jīngyàn

experienced

聪明
cōngmíng

smart

有威信
yǒu wēixìn

prestigious

NOTES

Statistics from China Securities Regulatory Commission showed that by the end of July 2006, there are 1379 listed companies in China (A or B share). The companies total market capitalization was RMB 4,745.968 billion, their negotiable market capitalization RMB 1,600.741 billion, and their total capital was 1,054.030 billion shares.

公司有多少个部门？

Gōngsī yǒu duōshao gè bùmén?

How many departments are there in the company?

● 公司有多少个部门？

Gōngsī yǒu duōshao gè bùmén?

● 包括财务部在内，一共

Bāokuò cáiwùbù zàinèi, yígòng

有 8 个部门。

yǒu bā gè bùmén.

● How many departments are there in the company?

● Including the Financial Department, there are eight departments in the company.

公司有多少个_____?
gōngsī yǒu duōshao gè

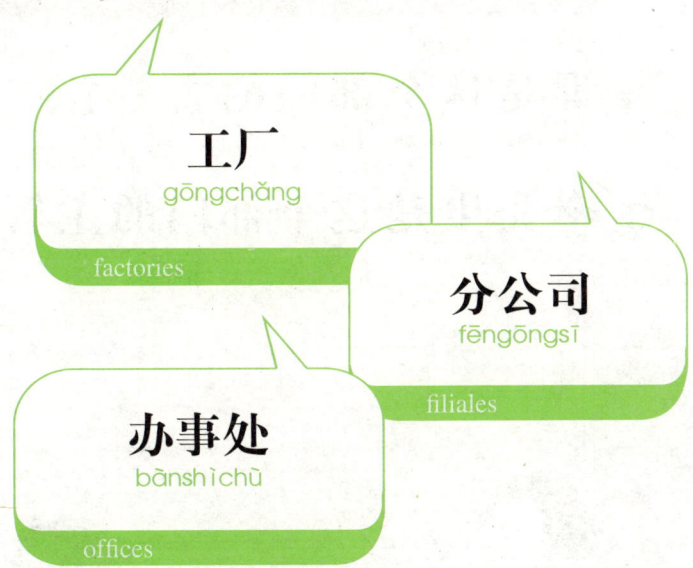

工厂
gōngchǎng

factories

分公司
fēngōngsī

filiales

办事处
bànshìchù

offices

A company usually includes a human resources department, general accounting department, sales department, public relations department, advertising department, planning department, and research and development department.

谁是这个部门的主管?
Shuí shì zhège bùmén de zhǔguǎn?

Who is in charge of this department?

● 谁是这个部门的**主管**?
Shuí shì zhège bùmén de zhǔguǎn?

● 李先生是这个部门的主管。
Lǐ xiānsheng shì zhège bùmén de zhǔguǎn.

外联部

○ Who is in charge of this department?
● Mr. Li is in charge of this department.

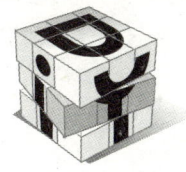

谁 是 这 个 部 门 的 _____?
shuí shì zhège bùmén de

负责人
fùzérén

person in charge

经理
jīnglǐ

manager

As the manager of a department, he has to make it clear what his staff are expected to do, as well as what results are expected, when he makes his assignments. When the person in charge is discussing the expected results with his staff, he should describe the results with visual, audible and tangible means, so that his ideas are truly understood.

我在客户服务部工作。
Wǒ zài kèhù fúwùbù gōngzuò.

I work in the Customer Service Department.

● 你在哪个部门工作？
Nǐ zài nǎge bùmén gōngzuò?

● 我在客户服务部工作。
Wǒ zài kèhù fúwùbù gōngzuò.

客户服务部

● What department do you work in?
● I work in the Customer Service Department.

我 在 ＿＿＿＿＿＿＿＿＿工 作 。
wǒ zài   gōngzuò

人力资源部
rénlì zīyuánbù

Human Resources Department

总经理办公室
zǒngjīnglǐ bàngōngshì

Office of the General Manager

技术部
jìshùbù

Technical Department

NOTES

Quality customers have always been the focus of competition in the banking circle. Banks depend on their services to retain their customers. By giving a detailed introduction of the function of the Customer Service Department and its service scope for VIP customers, banks will help people understand the department. That is why the publicity of customer services is so important.

青岛啤酒集团在国内有多家子公司。

Qīngdǎo píjiǔ jítuán zài guónèi yǒu duō jiā zǐgōngsī.

Tsingtao Brewery Group has several subsidiary companies nationwide.

● 青岛啤酒集团的规模不小吧？

Qīngdǎo píjiǔ jítuán de guīmó bù xiǎo ba?

● 青岛啤酒集团在国内有多家

Qīngdǎo píjiǔ jítuán zài guónèi yǒu duō jiā

子公司。

zǐgōngsī.

● The scale of the Tsingtao Brewery Group is rather big, isn't it?

● Tsingtao Brewery Group has several subsidiary companies nationwide.

青岛啤酒集团在＿＿＿＿＿有
qīngdǎo píjiǔ jítuán zài   yǒu
多家子公司。
duō jiā zǐgōngsī

海外
hǎiwài

overseas

全球
quánqiú

around the globe

华东地区
huádōng dìqū

in East China

NOTES

Tsingtao Brewery Group is usually abbreviated as "Tsingtao". Its predecessor is a brewery company established in Qingdao in 1903 by British and Germany merchants. China's brewery industry has been growing at a high rate of 30% annually since 1979. China is now indeed a big country both in production and consumption.

全球有6万名员工为这家跨国公司工作。

Quánqiú yǒu liù wàn míng yuángōng wèi zhè jiā kuàguó gōngsī gōngzuò.

There are 60,000 employees working for this multinational company around the globe.

● 这家跨国公司的员工有

Zhè jiā kuàguó gōngsī de yuángōng yǒu

多少人？

duōshao rén?

● 全球有6万名员工为这家

Quánqiú yǒu liù wàn míng yuángōng wèi zhè jiā

跨国公司工作。

kuàguó gōngsī gōngzuò.

● How many employees work for this multinational company?

● There are 60,000 employees working for this multinational company around the globe.

_____有 6 万名员工
yǒu liù wàn míng yuángōng
为这家跨国公司工作。
wèi zhè jiā kuàguó gōngsī gōngzuò

全国
quánguó

nationwide

东北地区
dōngběi dìqū

in the Northeast

NOTES

In the 1980s, multinational companies introduced advanced products, equipments and other hardware into China. In the 1990s, they introduced the modern corporate system into China. In the 21st century, they have introduced the latest concept of enterprise management into China. Multinational companies have become a proactive element in the sustainable development of China by introducing enterprise hardware, enterprise systems and relevant concepts.

可口可乐公司总部在亚特兰大。

Kěkǒu kělè gōngsī zǒngbù zài Yàtèlándà.

The Coca-Cola Company is based in Atlanta.

● 可口可乐公司总部在哪儿？

Kěkǒu kělè gōngsī zǒngbù zài nǎr?

◐ 可口可乐公司总部在亚特兰大。

Kěkǒu kělè gōngsī zǒngbù zài Yàtèlándà.

● Where is The Coca-Cola Company based?

◐ The Coca-Cola Company is based in Atlanta.

公司＿＿＿＿＿＿＿＿＿＿在
gōngsī   zài

亚特兰大。
Yàtèlándà

生产基地
shēngchǎn jīdì

Production Base

研发中心
yánfā zhōngxīn

Research and Development Center

原料产地
yuánliào chǎndì

raw material production area

NOTES

Coca-Cola is one of the most welcome soft drinks in the Chinese market. By 2004, The Coca-Cola Company's investment in China reached US $ 1.2 billion; the Coca-Cola system includes 29 bottling companies and 32 factory buildings in the Chinese Mainland. 98% of its raw material is purchased from China. At present, the Coca-Cola system in China has about 20,000 employees, among which 99% are local Chinese.

董事会任命了新的首席执行官。

Dǒngshìhuì rènmìng le xīn de shǒuxí zhí.xíngguān.

The Board of Directors appointed a new Chief Executive Officer.

● 董事会做了什么决定？

Dǒngshìhuì zuò le shénme juédìng?

● 董事会任命了新的首席

Dǒngshìhuì rènmìng le xīn de shǒuxí

执行官。

zhíxíngguān.

董事局会议

● What decision did the Board of Directors make?

● The Board of Directors appointed a new Chief Executive Officer.

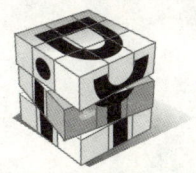

董事会任命了新的

dǒngshìhuì rènmìng le xīn de

————————————。

首席财务官

shǒuxí cáiwùguān

Chief Financial Officer

首席信息官

shǒuxí xìnxīguān

Chief Information Officer

常务副总裁

chángwù fù zǒngcái

Executive Vice President

NOTES

Chief Executive Officers in Chinese enterprises who are comparatively renown include Zhang Ruimin of Haier Group, Yang Lianqing of Lenovo Group, and Zhang Chaoyang of Sohu Company.

这是我们公司的电子名片。

Zhè shì wǒmen gōngsī de diànzǐ míngpiàn.

This is our company's electronic name card.

● 这是我们公司的电子名片。

Zhè shì wǒmen gōngsī de diànzǐ míngpiàn.

● 谢谢！

Xièxie!

● This is our company's electronic name card.
● Thank you!

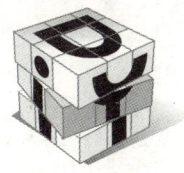

这是我们公司的＿＿＿＿＿＿。
zhè shì wǒmen gōngsī de

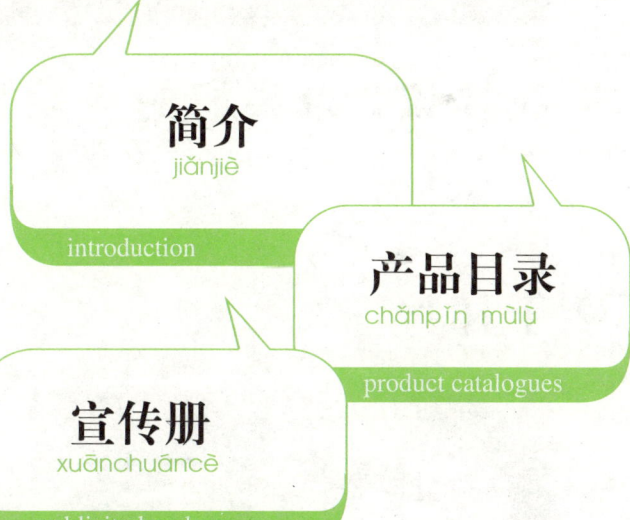

简介
jiǎnjiè

introduction

产品目录
chǎnpǐn mùlù

product catalogues

宣传册
xuānchuáncè

publicity brochure

NOTE

Electronic name cards are a standardized online file transmission format. They transmit the information on traditional paper business cards over the internet in a standardized format. Electronic name cards are widely used. Users can easily read and forward the information on those cards by directly sending emails and other means.

我提议，为我们的 成功 合作干杯！
Wǒ tíyì, wèi wǒmen de chénggōng hézuò gānbēi!

May I propose a toast to our successful cooperation!

● **我提议，为我们的成功合作**
Wǒ tíyì, wèi wǒmen de chénggōng hézuò
干杯！
gānbēi!

● **干杯！**
Gānbēi!

● May I propose a toast to our successful cooperation!
● Cheers!

我 提 议 ， 为 _____ 干 杯 ！
wǒ tíyì wèi gānbēi

我们的新合同
wǒmen de xīn hétong

our new contract

这次会面
zhè cì huìmiàn

this meeting

大家的身体健康
dàjiā de shēntǐ jiànkāng

our health

NOTES

Guests are addressed as "distinguished guests" in a toast speech at a reception to express thanks. People usually say "I wish you good health", "I wish your family happiness", "I wish you smooth sailing in your work", "I wish you flourishing business", or "I wish you all the best", when proposing a toast.

欢迎代表团参观我们的工厂！

Huānyíng dàibiǎotuán cānguān wǒmen de gōngchǎng!

We welcome the delegation to visit our factory!

● 欢迎代表团参观我们的
Huānyíng dàibiǎotuán cānguān wǒmen de
工厂！
gōngchǎng!

● 谢谢！ 这是我们的荣幸。
Xièxie! Zhè shì wǒmen de róngxìng.

● We welcome the delegation to visit our factory!
● Thank you. It's our honor.

欢迎代表团参观我们的

huānyíng dàibiǎotuán cānguān wǒmen de

_____!

车间
chējiān

workshop

产品陈列室
chǎnpǐn chénlièshì

product exhibition room

生产线
shēngchǎnxiàn

production line

NOTES

Visits to a company usually proceed in the following sequence: First the visiting delegation hears a general briefing from representatives of the factory. Then, accompanied by the representatives, the delegation visits the factory, commodity exhibition rooms and production workshop. They also communicate with the factory director on the sources of raw material, production line, equipment and relevant technology and other issues of their interest. As the visit draws to an end, a group photo is taken for both the visitors and the host.

今年博览会参展的厂商有多少？
Jīnnián   bólǎnhuì   cānzhǎn de chǎngshāng yǒu duōshao?

How many manufacturers attended this year's exposition?

● 今年 博览会 参展的厂商
   Jīnnián   bólǎnhuì   cānzhǎn de chǎngshāng

有多少？
yǒu duōshao?

● 据说有100多家。
   Jùshuō   yǒu   yìbǎi   duō jiā.

● How many manufacturers attended this year's exposition?

● It is said that more than 100 manufacturers attended this
   year's exposition.

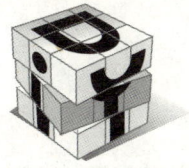

今年＿＿＿＿＿参展的厂商
jīnnián　　　　　　cānzhǎn de chǎngshāng

有多少？
yǒu duōshao

商品交易会
shāngpǐn jiāoyìhuì

commodity fair

展销会
zhǎnxiāohuì

exhibition and sales fair

NOTES

In 1999, 9.4 million people from 95 countries attended the World Horticultural Expo hosted by Kunming city of China's Yunnan Province. Shanghai will host the World Expo in 2010. Chinese people believe that World Expo Shanghai 2010 will be another successful, splendid and unforgettable event.

25

这个礼物代表我们的一点心意，请您收下。

Zhège lǐwù dàibiǎo wǒmen de yìdiǎn xīnyì, qǐng nín shōu xià.

This gift is a token of our appreciation. Please do accept it.

● 这个**礼物**代表我们的一点

　　Zhège　　lǐwù　dàibiǎo wǒmen de　yìdiǎn

心意，请您收下。

xīnyì,　　qǐng nín shōu xià.

● 谢谢！我们也准备了一些

　Xièxie!　　　Wǒmen　yě zhǔnbèi　le　　yìxiē

小礼品要送给你们。

xiǎo　lǐpǐn　yào sòng gěi　nǐmen.

● This gift is a token of our appreciation. Please accept it.

● Thank you! We also have some small gifts for you.

这个_____代表我们的一点
zhège　　　　dàibiǎo wǒmen de yìdiǎn

心意，请您收下。
xīnyì　　　qǐng nín shōu xià

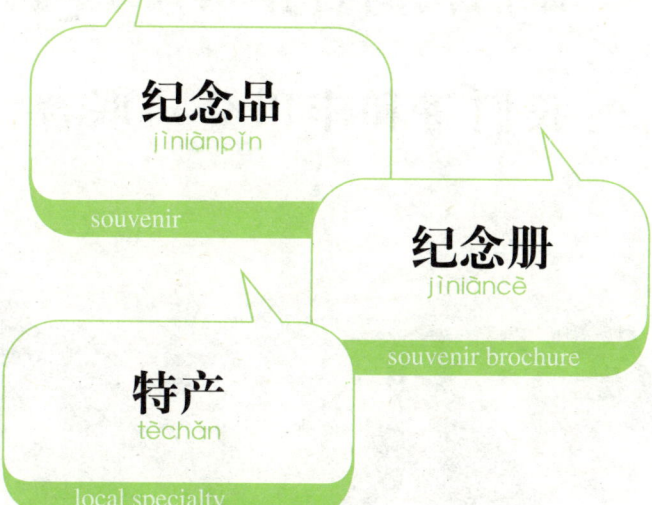

纪念品
jìniànpǐn

souvenir

纪念册
jìniàncè

souvenir brochure

特产
tèchǎn

local specialty

When conducting business, people sometimes present souvenirs with their companies' logo, gifts, or some special local products to show their respect to their counterparts. Chinese kites, Erhu, flutes, paper cuts, chopsticks, seals, facial Mask of Beijing Opera, calligraphy, drawings and tea can all serve as gifts to foreigners.

26

我们将和丰田公司联合开发新产品。

Wǒmen jiāng hé Fēngtián Gōngsī liánhé kāifā xīn chǎnpǐn.

We will jointly develop new products with the Toyota Company.

你们找到合作伙伴了吗？

Nǐmen zhǎodǎo hézuò huǒbàn le ma?

我们将和丰田公司联合

Wǒmen jiāng hé Fēngtián Gōngsī liánhé

开发新产品。

kāifā xīn chǎnpǐn.

Have you found your joint venture partners?

We will jointly develop new products with the Toyota Company.

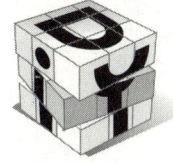

我们将和丰田公司联合
wǒmen jiāng hé Fēngtiān Gōngsī liánhé

_____ 。

推广新业务
tuīguǎng xīn yèwù

promote our new business

举行新闻发布会
jǔxíng xīnwén fābùhuì

hold a press conference

收购XX公司
shōugòu gōngsī

acquire ×× company

NOTES

In China, Toyota has a joint venture with First Automotive Works in Tianjin, Chengdu and Changchun in automobile production, as well as a joint venture with Guangzhou Automobile Industry Group. In addition, it also has proactive and broad exchange and cooperation with China in automobile technology and other fields.

27

请允许我代表大家向您表示感谢!

Qǐng yǔnxǔ wǒ dàibiǎo dàjiā xiàng nín biǎoshì gǎnxiè!

Please allow me, on behalf of all of us, to express our gratitude to you!

● 请允许我代表大家向您
Qǐng yǔnxǔ wǒ dàibiǎo dàjiā xiàng nín
表示感谢!
biǎoshì gǎnxiè!

● 您太客气了!
Nín tài kèqi le!

● Please allow me, on behalf of all of us, to express our gratitude to you!
● You really flatter me!

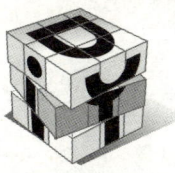

请允许我代表_____向
qǐng yǔnxǔ wǒ dàibiǎo   xiàng

您表示感谢！
nín biǎoshì gǎnxiè

公司
gōngsī

our company

同事们
tóngshìmen

our colleagues

董事会
dǒngshìhuì

the Board of Directors

NOTES

The following are some expressions to express gratitude: "First of all, please allow me, on behalf of the ABC Company, to express our heartfelt gratitude to you." or "Please allow me, on behalf my colleagues, to express our heartfelt gratitude for ABC Company's warm hospitality." "We have achieved… in such a short time. All should be attributed to your sincere cooperation and strong support, for which we wish to express our heartfelt gratitude."

28

我如何与您取得联系?
Wǒ rúhé yǔ nín qǔdé liánxì?

How can I contact you?

● 我 如何 与 您 取得联系?
Wǒ rúhé yǔ nín qǔdé liánxì?

● 你 可以 发 邮件 或 打 电话。
Nǐ kěyǐ fā yóujiàn huò dǎ diànhuà.

○ How can I contact you?
○ You can send me an email or call me.

56

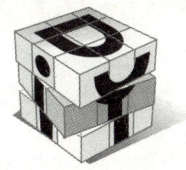

我如何与您_____?
wǒ rúhé yǔ nín

及时沟通
jíshí gōutōng

communicate with
you promptly

保持联系
bǎochí liánxì

keep in touch with you

There are various uses for a name card. It provides essential information needed for future contact; it makes it possible for people to focus on their exchange when they first meet, rather than just focus on memorizing each other's personal information. It also polishes people's behavior in their meeting, making it possible to avoid embarrassment when one attempts to introduce himself to the other. In today's fast-paced times, it can even take the place of a formal visit.

29

希望你们能给我们介绍新的合作伙伴！
Xīwàng nǐmen néng gěi wǒmen jièshào xīn de hézuò huǒbàn!
We hope that you will introduce new partners to us!

● 还需要我们做什么吗？
Hái xūyào wǒmen zuò shénme ma?

● 希望你们能给我们介绍新
Xīwàng nǐmen néng gěi wǒmen jièshào xīn

的合作伙伴！
de hézuò huǒbàn!

合作
伙伴

● Is there anything we can do for you?
● We hope that you will introduce new partners to us!

希望你们能给我们介绍
xīwàng nǐmen néng gěi wǒmen jièshào

新的 _____ !
xīn de

合伙人
héhuǒrén

partners

项目
xiàngmù

projects

客户
kèhù

customers

NOTES

The partners of the Beijing 2008 Olympic Games are Bank of China, China Network Communications Group Corporation, China Petrochemical Corporation, China National Petroleum Corporation, China Mobile Communications Corporation, Volkswagen Group China, Johnson & Johnson (China) Investment Ltd, adidas, Air China Limited, and so on.

30

公司将举办战略合作伙伴答谢会。

Gōngsī jiāng jǔbàn zhànlüè hézuō huǒbàn dǎxiēhuì.

The company will hold a reception of thanks for our strategic partners.

● 公司近期有什么会务安排
Gōngsī jìnqī yǒu shénme huìwù ānpái
吗？
ma?

● 公司将举办战略合作伙伴
Gōngsī jiāng jǔbàn zhànlüè hézuō huǒbàn
答谢会。
dǎxiēhuì.

● What are the company's latest meeting plans?
● The company will hold a reception of thanks for our strategic partners.

公司将举办＿＿＿＿＿＿＿。
gōngsī jiāng jǔbàn

年终员工感谢会
niánzhōng yuángōng gǎnxièhuì

a year-end reception to thank employees

记者招待会
jìzhě zhāodàihuì

a press conference

新产品推介会
xīn chǎnpǐn tuī jiè huì

new production promotion

China's renowned local brand in sporting goods Li Ning, has become the NBA's strategic partner. The Li Ning brand will then be closely connected with the globally influential NBA and its players. Basketball and other related events of the Li Ning brand will appear on the official website of NBA and at NBA matches broadcast live nationwide.

31

公司投入了8000万人民币进行新产品研发。

Gōngsī tóurù le bā qiānwàn rénmínbì jìnxíng xīn chǎnpǐn yánfā.

The company has invested 80 million RMB in the research and development of new products.

● 新产品的研发投入了多少

Xīn chǎnpǐn de yánfā tóurù le duōshao

资金？

zījīn?

● 公司投入了8000万人民币

Gōngsī tóurù le bā qiānwǎn rénmínbì

进行新产品研发。

jìnxíng xīn chǎnpǐn yánfā.

研发部

● How much has been invested in the research and development of new products?

● The company has invested 80 million RMB in the research and development of new products.

公司投入了＿＿＿＿＿人民币
gōngsī tóurù le rénmínbì

进行新产品研发。
jìnxíng xīn chǎnpǐn yánfā

几十万
jǐshí wàn

hundreds of thousands

100万
yì bǎiwàn

1 million

1亿
yí yì

100 million

NOTES

In English, commas are used in figures bigger than 1,000. Count three from right to left and use one comma in each instance, then the commas will represent thousand, million, billion etc., respectively, from right to left. In Chinese, however, one has to count four when dividing similar units in a figure; thus 549,946,746 will be divided by vertical strokes as 5|49,94|6,746, and the vertical stroke will then represent wan (ten thousand), yi (100 million), from right to left. Thus the above figure would be read WU (5) YI SI (4) QIAN (thousand) JIU (9) BAI (hundred) JIUSHISI (94) WAN LIU (6) QIAN QI (7) BAI LIUSHIBA (68).

王选发明了汉字激光照排系统。
Wáng Xuǎn fāmíng le hànzì jīguāng zhàopái xìtǒng.

Wang Xuan invented a computerized laser photocomposition system for Chinese character typesetting.

● 谁发明了汉字激光照排系统？
　Shuí fāmíng le hànzì jīguāng zhàopái xìtǒng?

● 王选发明了汉字激光照排
　Wáng Xuǎn fāmíng le hànzì jīguāng zhàopái

系统。
xìtǒng.

● Who invented the computerized laser photocomposition system for Chinese character typesetting?

● Wang Xuan invented a computerized laser photocomposition system for Chinese character typesetting.

古代中国人发明了
gǔdài Zhōngguórén fāmíng le

_____。

造纸术
zàozhǐshù

paper making

指南针
zhǐnánzhēn

the mariner's compass

印刷术
yìnshuāshù

printing

火药
huǒyào.

gunpowder

Professor Wang Xuan (1937—2006) of Peking University devoted himself to the research of the computerized processing of words (Chinese characters), graphics and images. He has acquired one European patent and eight Chinese patents. The industrialization and application of the above achievements has promoted the technical revolution of China's newspaper, printing and publishing industries. Prof. Wang Xuan also proposed and led the research and development of computerized laser photocomposition system for colored Chinese character typesetting, helping China's newspaper technology and its application to rank the best in the world.

33

公司有100多项国家专利。

Gōngsī yǒu yìbǎi duō xiàng guójiā zhuānlì.

The company has more than 100 patents in the country.

● 贵公司的专利拥有情况

Guì gōngsī de zhuānlì yōngyǒu qíngkuàng

怎么样？

zěnmeyàng?

● 公司有100多项国家专利。

Gōngsī yǒu yìbǎi duō xiàng guójiā zhuānlì.

○ How is patent portfolio of your company?

● Our company has more than 100 patents in the country.

公司有100多项_____。
gōngsī yǒu yìbǎi duō xiàng

技术专利
jìshù zhuānlì

technical patent

实用新型专利
shíyòng xīnxíng zhuānlì

patent of practical new application

国际专利
guójì zhuānlì

international patents

NOTES

The Commercial Law promulgated in 1982 is the first law on intellectual property rights in the Chinese Mainland, and was a symbol for the establishment of China's Intellectual Property Rights Protection System. The promulgation of the Patent Law in 1984 and the Copyright Law in 1990 symbolized the primary formation of China's Intellectual Property Rights Protection System.

34

新产品将在新年前投放当地市场。

Xīn chǎnpǐn jiāng zài xīnnián qián tóufàng dāngdì shìchǎng.

New products will be launched in the local market before the new year.

● 新产品什么时候投放市场？

Xīn chǎnpǐn shénme shíhòu tóufàng shìchǎng?

● 新产品将在新年前投放

Xīn chǎnpǐn jiāng zài xīnnián qián tóufàng

当地市场。

dāngdì shìchǎng.

● When will the new products be launched in the local market?

● New products will be launched in the local market before the new year.

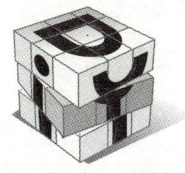

新产品将在新年前投放
xīn chǎnpǐn jiāng zài xīnnián qián tóufàng

＿＿＿＿＿＿市场。
shìchǎng

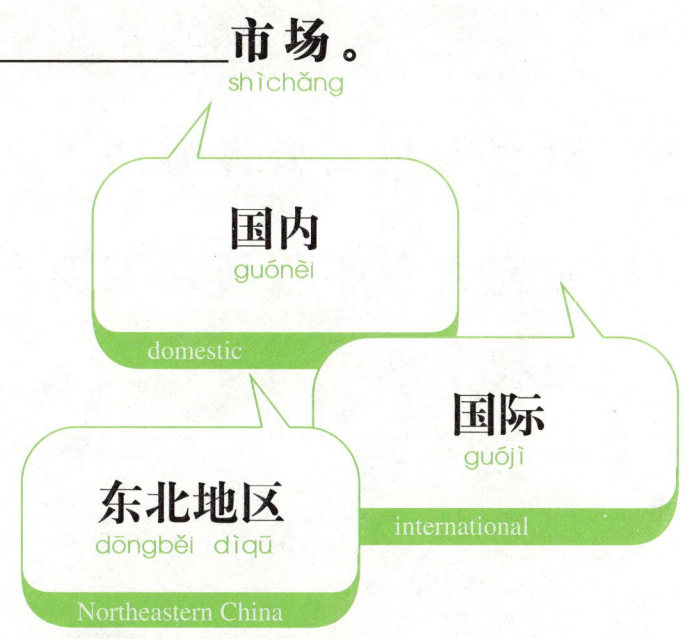

国内
guónèi

domestic

国际
guójì

international

东北地区
dōngběi dìqū

Northeastern China

When new products make their debut in the market, advertisements will focus on introducing the characteristics and usage of them, so as to inspire consumers' demand in hopes that customers will deem it a glory to possess these "top grade" consumables. That will in turn stimulate their desire to buy the products, thereby promoting the purchase and consumption of the new products. Therefore, launching new products just before festivals and holidays helps to increase sale volume.

35

研究人员不仅要研发新产品，还要了解市场变化。
Yánjiū rényuán bùjǐn yào yánfā xīn chǎnpǐn, háiyào liǎojiě shìchǎng biànhuà.

Researchers not only develop new products, they must also be aware of market changes.

○ 研究人员需要做哪些工作？
Yánjiū rényuán xūyào zuò nǎxiē gōngzuò?

● 研究人员不仅要研发新产品，
Yánjiū rényuán bùjǐn yào yánfā xīn chǎnpǐn,

还要了解市场变化。
háiyào liǎojiě shìchǎng biànhuà.

○ What are researchers required to do?
● Researchers not only develop new products, they must also be aware of market changes.

研究人员不仅要研发新产品，
yánjiū rényuán bùjǐn yào yánfā xīn chǎnpǐn,

还要了解＿＿＿＿＿＿＿＿＿。
hǎiyào liǎojiě

时代需求
shídài xūqiú

current demands

消费人群
xiāofèi rénqún

consumer groups

原材料价格
yuáncáiliào jiàgé

prices of raw materials

NOTES

Better off and higher income people are very concerned about the elevation of their quality of life; their consumption tendency also changes accordingly, with an increasing sense of making investments. Investigations have found that more and more high-income people are pursuing spiritual needs, education, culture, communication, health and housing as hot-spots of consumption. There is an increasingly tendency to pursue fashion and individuality. That is why researchers of an enterprise must be aware of the needs of consumers.

36

松下电器在中国还生产洗衣机。

Sōngxià Diànqì zài Zhōngguó hái shēngchǎn xǐyījī.

Panasonic Electronics also produces washing machines in China.

● 除了电视机，松下电器
Chúle diànshìjī, Sōngxià Diànqì

在中国还生产什么产品？
zài Zhōngguó hái shēngchǎn shénme chǎnpǐn?

● 松下电器在中国还生产
Sōngxià Diànqì zài Zhōngguó hái shēngchǎn

洗衣机。
xǐyījī.

○ What does Panasonic Electronics produce in China besides television sets?

● Panasonic Electronics also produces washing machines in China.

松下电器在中国生产
Sōngxià Diànqì zài Zhōngguó shēngchǎn

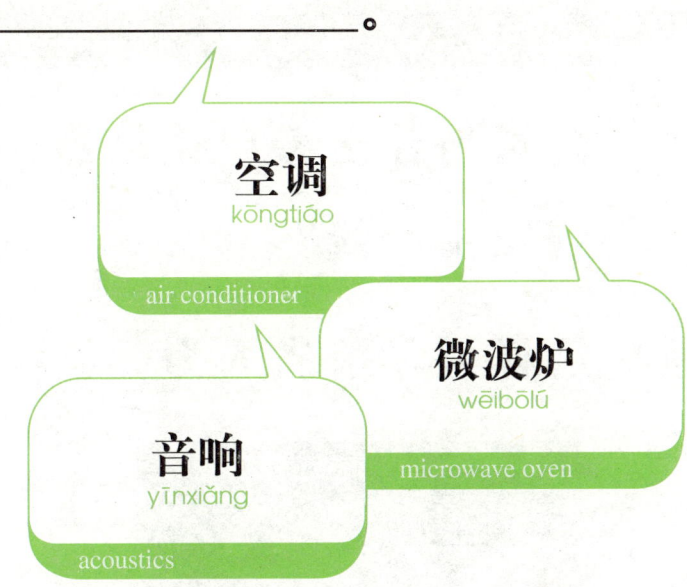

空调
kōngtiáo

air conditioner

微波炉
wēibōlú

microwave oven

音响
yīnxiǎng

acoustics

Panasonic Electronics exported its products to China beginning in 1978. In September, 1987, Panasonic Electronics established its first joint venture in China (Beijing). After that, it subsequently established companies funded by itself or joint ventures in areas ranging from home appliances like air conditioners and washing machines to communication equipment. The number of such ventures reached 61 by December 31, 2004. Its products have won great praise.

37

公司为什么希望让机器人管理生产线?

Gōngsī wèishénme xīwàng ràng jīqìrén guǎnlǐ shēngchǎnxiàn?

Why does the company wish to have robots run the production lines?

● 公司为什么希望让机器人

　Gōngsī wèishénme xīwàng ràng jīqìrén

　管理生产线?

　guǎnlǐ shēngchǎnxiàn?

● 这样可以节省人力。

　Zhèyàng kěyǐ jiéshěng rénlì.

● Why does the company wish to have robots run the production lines?

● So that manpower can be saved.

公司为什么希望让_____
gōngsī wèishénme xīwàng ràng

管理生产线？
guǎnlǐ shēngchǎnxiǎn

技术人员
jìshù rényuán

technicians

工程师
gōngchéngshī

engineers

外国专家
wàiguó zhuānjiā

foreign experts

NOTES

The research of developing a robot is a personating process from the very beginning. That was why development and manufacture of manipulators occurs — so that machines can be used to replace labors and explorations in which human being would fail. However, in the last decade or so, the development of robots is not only improving all the time, but its application has also covered many fields — industry, agriculture, inheritance bio industry, iatrology, cultural industry, communication sector, energy exploration, industry revolution in all these fields will emerge due to the enormous launch of robots.

38

由于自动化技术的发展，工人的工作轻松多了。

Yóuyú zìdònghuà jìshù de fāzhǎn, gōngrén de gōngzuò qīngsōng duō le.

Workers' work has considerably eased due to the development of automation technology.

● **为什么工人的工作比以前**
Wèishénme gōngrén de gōngzuò bǐ yǐqián

轻松了？
qīngsōng le?

● **由于自动化技术的发展，**
Yóuyú zìdònghuà jìshù de fāzhǎn,

工人的工作轻松多了。
gōngrén de gōngzuò qīngsōng duō le.

● Why is workers' work easier than before?

● Workers' work has considerably eased due to the development of automation technology.

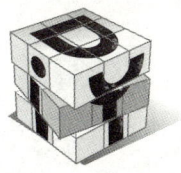

由于_____技术的发展，
yóuyú   jìshù de fāzhǎn,

工人的工作轻松多了。
gōngrén de gōngzuò qīngsōng duō le

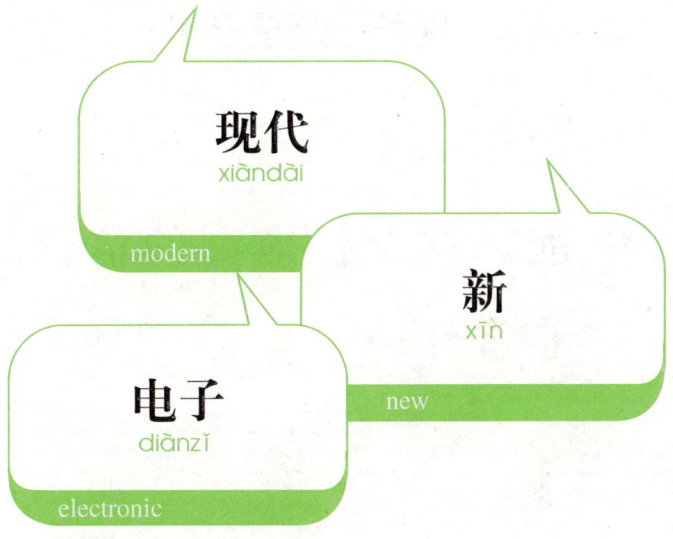

现代
xiàndài

modern

新
xīn

new

电子
diǎnzǐ

electronic

NOTES

With the spread of computers, people have introduced a system of automatic control of beer production process, so as to avoid the mistakes of human operations. Automatic control has sufficient flexibility and great headways have been made in the accuracy of the control process. Effective saving of historical data of the production process also provides good raw data as reference for the factory to conduct analysis on the control process, thus promoting the quality of products.

39

供应商能保证及时送货吗?

Gōngyìngshāng néng bǎozhèng jíshí sōnghuò ma?

Can the supplier assure that those goods could be delivered on time?

● 供应商能保证及时送货

Gōngyìngshāng néng bǎozhèng jíshí sōnghuò

吗?

ma?

● 能，这个供应商的信誉

Néng, zhège gōngyìngshāng de xìnyù

非常好。

fēicháng hǎo.

○ Can the supplier guarantee that those goods could be delivered on time?

● Yes, it can. This supplier enjoys good reputation.

供应商能保证及时

gōngyìngshāng néng bǎozhèng jíshí

_____吗？

ma

供货
gōnghuò
provide goods

补货
bǔhuò
supplement goods

上门维护
shàngmén wéihù
visiting maintenance

NOTES

In the past, what foreign buyers favored were competitive prices, quality and prompt delivery of goods. But in recent several years, something has changed in consumer behavior, and what they pondered about have added, among which their demand for an increase of added value is a striking one. It includes after service, advertisement support, clearance support and cultural identification.

40

无存货管理能降低生产成本。
Wúcúnhuò guǎnlǐ néng jiāngdī shēngchǎn chéngběn.

Non-stock management reduces production costs.

● 怎么能降低生产成本？
　 Zěnme néng jiāngdī shēngchǎn chéngběn?

● 无存货管理能降低生产
　 Wúcúnhuò guǎnlǐ néng jiāngdī shēngchǎn

　 成本。
　 chéngběn.

● How could production costs be reduced?
● Non-stock management reduces production costs.

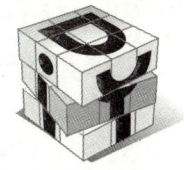

_____能 降 低
                 néng   jiàngdī

生 产 成 本 。
shēngchǎn chéngběn

高科技的使用
gāokējì　de shǐyòng

application of hi-tech

新材料的应用
xīncáiliào　de yìngyòng

application of new material

NOTES

Stock in trade refers to the material of an enterprise reserved for sales or consumption in its production and operation process. It usually includes different kinds of raw material, fuel, packing material, etc. The so-called non-stock management refers to such a situation in which the supplier will not send accessories or raw material in until they are needed in the manufacturers' production process. This way the manufacturers can lower their costs.

41

这家超市的商品价廉物美。

Zhè jiā chāoshì de shāngpǐn jiàlián wùměi.

Goods in this supermarket are nice and cheap.

● 这家超市的商品怎么样？
Zhè jiā chāoshì de shāngpǐn zěnmeyàng?

● 这家超市的商品价廉物美。
Zhè jiā chāoshì de shāngpǐn jiàlián wùměi.

● How are the goods in this supermarket?
● Goods in this supermarket are nice and cheap.

这 家 ＿＿＿＿ 的 商 品 价 廉 物 美 。
zhè jiā　　　　　de shāngpǐn jiǎlián wǔměi

连锁店
liánsuǒdiàn

chain store

便利店
biànlìdiàn

store

商场
shāngchǎng

emporium

NOTES

Carrefour, a multinational chain enterprise, entered China first by taking a joint-venture in 1995. By the end of 2005, Carrefour opened 60 large-scale supermarkets in 20 cities around China.

In 1996, Wal-mart from the U.S., METRO Group from Germany, Ito Yokado from Japan, Lotus from Thailand and other large–scale multinational chain retail enterprises also opened many shops in China, and are sourcing locally.

42

这款手机的定价很低，很有市场竞争力。

Zhè kuǎn shǒujī de dìngjià hěn dī, hěn yǒu shìchǎng jìngzhēng lì.

This cell phone has been set at a very low price. It is highly competitive in the market.

● 这款手机的定价怎么样？

Zhè kuǎn shǒujī de dìngjià zěnmeyàng?

● 这款手机的定价很低，很

Zhè kuǎn shǒujī de dìngjià hěn dī, hěn

有市场竞争力。

yǒu shìchǎng jìngzhēng lì.

○ How is the price of this cell phone?

● This cell phone has been set at a very low price. It is highly competitive in the market.

84

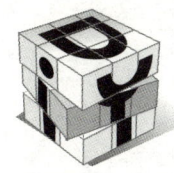

这款手机的＿＿＿＿＿＿＿，
zhè kuǎn shǒujī de

很有市场竞争力。
hěn yǒu shìchǎng jìngzhēng lì

款式很时尚
kuǎnshì hěn shíshàng

fashionable in style

功能很多
gōngnéng hěnduō

diversified in function

NOTES

Price setting of a commodity will take costs and profit into account, and the acceptance capability of local consumers as well. In order to attract consumers, shops often cross the original printed price in red, and put a new, hand-written price in yellow. The price will then look more attractive.

43

节日期间的促销活动真不少。

Jiérì qījiān de cùxiāo huódòng zhēn bù shǎo.

There are so many promotion events during the holidays.

● 这个"十一"买了不少东西吧？

zhège "shíyī" mǎi le bù shǎo dōngxi ba?

● 节日期间的促销活动真不少，

Jiérì qījiān de cùxiāo huódòng zhēn bù shǎo,

我已经买了很多东西了。

wǒ yǐjīng mǎi le hěnduō dōngxi le.

十一大促销！

● You must have done a lot of shopping during the National Day holiday?

● There are so many promotion events during the holidays. I have bought many things already.

节日期间的＿＿＿＿活动真不少。
jiérì　qījiān　de　　　huódòng zhēn bù shǎo

优惠
yōuhuì

preferential price

特卖
tè mài

sales

打折
dǎzhé

discount

NOTES

In a broader sense, promotion of sales, or promotion, refers to advertisement, public relations and ground promotion events which all help promote the sales of a certain product. While in a narrower sense, only activities which promote sales volume can be defined as promotion. Therefore, the objectives, timing, means and other strategies of a promotion will all matter.

44

青岛啤酒的市场份额在不断增加。

Qīngdǎo píjiǔ de shìchǎng fēn'é zài búduàn zēngjiā.

The market share of Tsingtao Beer is at a constant rise.

● 在国外的超市能买到青岛

Zài guówài de chāoshì néng mǎi dào qīngdǎo

啤酒吗？

píjiǔ ma?

● 能买到，青岛啤酒的市场

Néng mǎi dào, qīngdǎo píjiǔ de shìchǎng

份额在不断增加。

fēn'é zài búduàn zēngjiā.

● Can one buy Tsingtao Beer in the supermarket overseas?

● It can be bought. The market share of the Tsingtao Beer is at a constant rise.

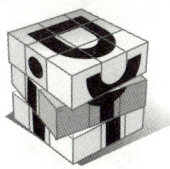

青岛啤酒的 _____ 在
qīngdǎo píjiǔ de   zài

不断增加。
búduàn zēngjiā

销售量
xiāoshòu liàng

sales volume

销售收入
xiāoshòu shōurù

sales income

广告投入
guǎnggào tóurù

advertisement input

NOTES

The concept of market share first originated in the U.S. in the 1960s, and was soon spread worldwide, becoming the analytical tool which marketing managers and enterprise managers have special interests and use frequently. However, it will be wrong if one pursues market share only, as, firstly, market shares acquired from fighting a pricing war would be difficult to maintain; and secondly, even if such market shares could be maintained, long-term profit is uncertain, as the average profit rate within the circle will then descend constantly.

45

IBM 非常强调自己的市场导向性特点。

IBM　fēicháng qiǎngdiào zìjǐ　de shìchǎng dǎoxiàngxìng tèdiǎn.

IBM puts a strong emphasis on its characteristics of market-oriented.

● **IBM 非常强调自己的市场**
　　IBM　　fēicháng qiǎngdiào　zìjǐ　de　shìchǎng

导向性特点。
　dǎoxiàngxìng　tèdiǎn.

● **这也是他们成功的关键。**
　Zhè　yě　shì　tāmen chénggōng de　guānjiàn.

IBM产品发布会

● IBM puts a strong emphasis on its characteristics of market-oriented.

● That is also the key to their success.

IBM非常强调自己的 _____
IBM fēicháng qiángdiào zìjǐ de

特点。
tēdiǎn

服务
fúwù

service

安全
ānquán

security

高品质
gāo pǐnzhì

high quality

NOTES

The International Business Machine, or the IBM, was first initiated in 1911 in the U.S. It is the largest IT and operational solution company worldwide. It has more than 310,000 employees worldwide, and its business has spread to more than 160 countries and regions. The global taking of IBM reached US$96.5 billon in 2004. It transformed itself from a "technology-oriented" to "market-oriented" company in due time, and ensured the all-around demands of almost all users of different industries worldwide in information processing.

46

零售商的利润比批发商的高。
língshòushāng de lìrùn bǐ pīfāshāng de gāo.

Profit for retailers is higher than those of wholesalers.

● 零售商与批发商的利润
Língshòushāng yǔ pīfāshāng de lìrùn

一样吗？
yíyàng ma?

● 不一样，零售商的利润
Bù yíyàng, língshòushāng de lìrùn

比批发商的高。
bǐ pīfāshāng de gāo.

● Are the profits for retailers and wholesalers the same?
● No, they aren't. Profit for retailers is higher than those of the wholesalers.

零售商的利润比＿＿＿＿＿＿
língshòushāng de lìrùn bǐ

的高。
de gāo

代理商
dàilǐshāng

agents

制造商
zhìzàoshāng

manufacturers

供应商
gōngyìngshāng

suppliers

NOTES

There are so many sectors in retail business, their specific profit is not fixed. If a customer is familiar with a certain product, then profit could range from 0% to 10%. If a customer knows little about a certain product, then the profit range could go from 10% to 50%. But that varies depending on the different sectors. For instance, in department stores, many of the products there are daily commodities, their prices are transparent and the profit range is between 5% to 15%. In the medical industry, the profit of some new medicines could exceed 200%. The profit of computer products ranges from 10% to 30%, while for digital products it is a different story.

47

王先生一般什么时候拜访客户？

Wáng xiānsheng yìbān shénme shíhou bàifǎng kèhù?

When does Mr. Wang usually visit his customers?

○ 王先生一般什么时候 **拜访**
Wáng xiānsheng yìbān shénme shíhou bàifǎng

客户？
kèhù?

● 每年年底。
Měinián niándǐ.

某某有限公司

12月

1	2	3	4	5	6
7	8	9	10	11	12	13
14	15	16	17	18	19	20
21	22	23	24	25	26	27
28	29	30	31

○ When does Mr. Wang usually visit his clients?

● By the end of each year.

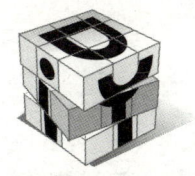

王先生一般什么时候＿＿＿＿
wǎng xiānsheng yìbān shénme shíhou

客户？
kèhù

看望
kànwàng

see

见
jiàn

meet

回访
huífǎng

pay return visit to

NOTES

Dealers do not make the purchase for themselves, but rather, they buy commodities from enterprises just to sell them. What they are interested in is the price difference instead of the actual price. For those enterprises, it is not account sale, as they get money from the dealers.

48

公司很看重自己的品牌形象。

Gōngsī hěn kànzhòng zìjǐ de pǐnpái xíngxiàng.

The company attaches much importance on its brand image.

○ **公司很看重产品质量吗？**

Gōngsī hěn kànzhòng chǎnpǐn zhìliàng ma?

● **当然，另外，公司也很看重**

Dāngrán, lìngwài, gōngsī yě hěn kànzhòng

自己的品牌形象。

zìjǐ de pǐnpái xíngxiàng.

○ Does the company attach much importance on the quality of its products?

● Of course it does. Besides, the company also attaches much importance on its brand image.

公司很看重自己的_____。
gōngsī hěn kānzhōng zìjǐ de

产品质量
chǎnpǐn zhìliàng

quality of products

市场份额
shìchǎng fèn'é

market share

企业文化
qǐyè wénhuà

enterprises culture

NOTES

In the Third Selection of "Most Valuable Brand" organized by Fortune (The Chinese Edition), Chinese companies like Haier (home appliance producer), Wuliangye and Maotai (both liquor producers), Lenovo (IT enterprise), Tongrentang (traditional Chinese medicine) and Tsingtao Beer were among those which ranked top 25.

49

降价销售是不是一种好的竞争策略？
Jiàngjià xiāoshòu shìbushì yīzhǒng hǎo de jìngzhēng cèlüè?

Is price-off promotion a good competition strategy?

- 降价销售是不是一种好的
  Jiàngjià xiāoshòu shìbushì yīzhǒng hǎo de

  竞争策略？
  jìngzhēng cèlüè?

- 不好说，这要视情况而定。
  Bù hǎo shuō, zhè yào shì qíngkuàng ér dìng.

- Is price-off promotion a good competition strategy?
- It's hard to say. It depends.

_____是不是一种
shìbushì yìzhǒng

好的竞争策略？
hǎo de jìngzhēng cèlüè

加大广告投入
jiādà guǎnggào tóurù

increasing adverti-
sement input

扩大宣传力度
kuòdà xuānchuán lìdù

strengthening publicity
efforts

增加供应链
zēngjiā gōngyìng liàn

increasing supply chains

The Law for Countering Unfair Competition stipulates that, "An operator shall not sell its or his goods at a price that is below the cost for the purpose of excluding its or his competitors."

50

网上商店的营业额每年都在增长。
Wǎng shàng shāngdiàn de yíngyè'é měi nián dōu zài zēngzhǎng.

The turnover of Internet shops is increasing year by year.

● 网上 商店的营业额大不大？
Wǎng shàng shāngdiàn de yíngyè'é dàbudà?

● 挺大的，而且网上商店的
Tǐng dà de, érqiě wǎng shàng shāngdiàn de

营业额每年都在增长。
yíngyè'é měi nián dōu zài zēngzhǎng.

● Do Internet shops have big turnovers?

● Yeah, and the turnover of Internet shops is increasing year by year.

网上 商店 的 ＿＿＿＿＿＿
wǎng shàng shāngdiàn de

每年都在增长。
měi nián dōu zài zēngzhǎng

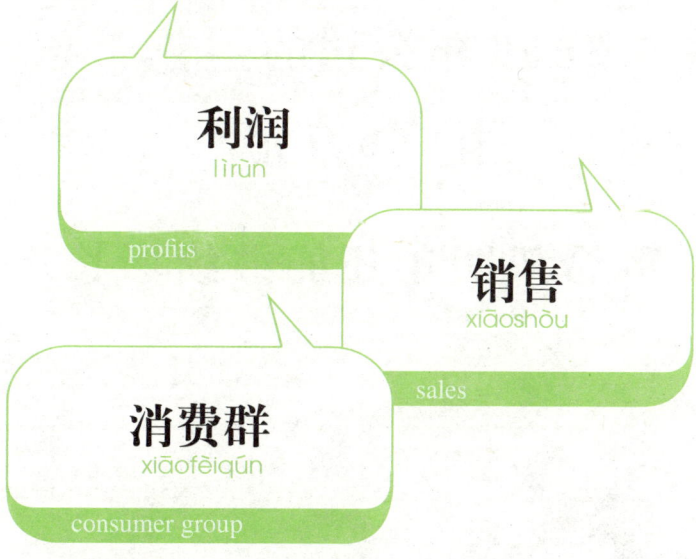

利润
lìrùn

profits

销售
xiāoshòu

sales

消费群
xiāofèiqún

consumer group

NOTES

Alibaba turned itself into the biggest internet trade market and business communication community worldwide in a short period. China's total volume in imports and exports were US$ 1 trillion, among which 1 million has been materialized through Alibaba. There are 13 million enterprises in China, among which 7 million are Alibaba customers. Alibaba was also named as one of the Best B2B Website of Asia by Forbes.

51

2006 年公司的主营业务收入有 800 万元。

Èrlínglíngliù nián gōngsī de zhǔyíng yèwù shōurù yǒu bābǎi wàn yuán.

The business revenue of the company in 2006 is RMB 8 million.

- **2006 年公司的主营业务**

  Èrlínglíngliù nián gōngsī de zhǔyíng yèwù

  收入有800万元。

  shōurù yǒu bābǎi wàn yuán.

- **希望明年还能继续增长。**

  Xīwàng míngnián hái néng jìxù zēngzhǎng.

- The business revenue of the company in 2006 is RMB 8 million.
- We hope it will continue to grow next year.

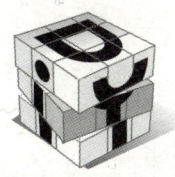

2006年公司的_____
èrlínglíngliù nián gōngsī de

有800万元。
yǒu bābǎi wàn yuán.

纯利润
chún lìrùn

net profit

全部收入
quánbù shōurù

total revenue

售后服务收入
shòuhòu fúwù shōurù

post-sale service revenue

NOTES

Business revenue is a general term applicable to all enterprises. With the development of economy, enterprises pluralized their business, which called for a term to express the meaning of main operations. Main business then emerged as a solution.

52

2006 年度公司的净利润是 120 万元。

Èrlínglíngliù niándù gōngsī de jìng lìrùn shì yìbǎi'èrshí wàn yuán.

The net profit of the company in 2006 is RMB 1.2 million.

● 去年公司的收入达到目标了吗？

Qùnián gōngsī de shōurù dádào mùbiāo le ma?

● 2006年度公司的净利润是 120万元，基本达到了目标。

Èrlínglíngliù niándù gōngsī de jìng lìrùn shì yìbǎi'èrshí wàn yuán, jīběn dádào le mùbiāo.

● Has the company achieved its goal in income last year?

● The net profit of the company in 2006 is RMB 1.2 million, and has reached its objective.

_____公司的净利润
　　　　　　　　gōngsī de jìng lìrùn
是120万元。
shì yìbǎi'èrshí wàn yuán.

第四季度
dì sì jìdù

the fourth quarter

上半年
shàngbànnián

first six months

NOTES

　　　　Net profit is what remains when due income tax is deducted from the total profit. It is the profit usable for the enterprises' actual distribution. The following is its formula: Total Profit—Income Tax=Net Profit

53

店主每个月要支付1万元的工资和3000元的租金。

Diànzhǔ měi gè yuè yào zhīfù yíwàn yuán de gōngzī hé sānqiān yuán de zūjīn.

The shop owner will have to pay RMB 10000 as salary and RMB 3000 as rent.

● 店主每个月的支出多不多？

Diàn zhǔ měi gè yuè de zhīchū duōbùduō?

● 店主每个月要支付1万元的

Diànzhǔ měi gè yuè yào zhīfù yíwàn yuán de

工资和3000元的租金。

gōngzī hé sānqiān yuán de zūjīn.

● Does the shop owner have to pay much each month?

● The shop owner will have to pay RMB 10000 as salary and RMB 3000 as rent.

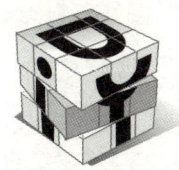

店主每个月要支付1万元的
diànzhǔ měi gè yuè yào zhīfù yí wàn yuán de

工资和3000元 的 _____。
gōngzī hé sānqiān yuán de

税金
shuìjīn

tax fees

材料费
cáiliàofèi

material fee

物业费
wùyèfèi

property management fee

If a shop owner wishes to employ an employee, the salary given to the employee depends on the local salary level, and will accounts for about 30-40% of his gross profit. Salary usually includes basic wages, bonus, subsidies and overtime wages, etc.

明年的预算计划你看了吗？

Míngnián de yùsuàn jǐhuà nǐ kàn le ma?

Have you seen next year's budget plan?

● 明年的预算计划你看了吗？

Míngnián de yùsuàn jǐhuà nǐ kàn le ma?

● 看过了，下午开会再讨论

Kànguò le, xiàwǔ kāihuì zài tǎolùn

一下。

yíxià.

● Have you seen next year's budget plan?

● Yes, I have. Let's discuss it during the afternoon meeting.

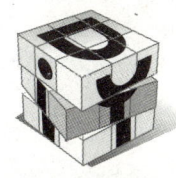

明年的 _____ 你看了吗？
míngnián de　　　　　　nǐ　kàn　le　ma

销售计划
xiāoshòu jìhuà
sales plan

宣传计划
xuānchuán jìhuà
promotion plan

广告计划
guǎnggào jìhuà
advertisement plan

NOTES

　　Master budget system include profit budget, capital expenditure balance budget, cash income and expenditure balance budget, assets-debt budget, cash flow budget and others.

55

你们怎么能减少研发经费呢?

Nǐmen zěnme néng jiǎnshǎo yánfā jīngfèi ne?

How could you reduce the Research and Development expenses?

● 你们怎么能减少研发经费呢?

Nǐmen zěnme néng jiǎnshǎo yánfā jīngfèi ne?

● 没办法，高层决定增加广告

Méi bànfǎ, gāocéng juédìng zēngjiā guǎnggào

费用。

fèiyòng.

● How could you reduce the Research and Development expenses?

● We can't do anything, as the higher authority has decided to increase advertisement expenses.

你们怎么能＿＿＿研发经费呢？
nǐmen zěnme néng　　　yánfā jīngfèi ne

削减
xuējiǎn
cut

挪用
nuóyòng
embezzle

浪费
làngfèi
waste

NOTES

One of the important conditions for maintaining the capability for independent imitativeness is to enjoy a strong input in scientific research. For example, the input in scientific research in Japanese enterprises has been increasing constantly from 1995, with total input in scientific research reached around JP¥ 16.8 billion each year. The scientific research input accounted for as high as 3.35% of its GDP.

56

公司必须控制生产成本。
Gōngsī bìxū kòngzhì shēngchǎn chéngběn.

The company must control its production cost.

- 公司必须控制生产成本。
  Gōngsī bìxū kòngzhì shēngchǎn chéngběn.

- 我同意，同时，也要控制
  Wǒ tóngyì, tóngshí, yě yào kòngzhì
  销售成本。
  xiāoshòu chéngběn.

- The company must control its production cost.
- I agree. Meanwhile, the company must control its sales cost.

公司必须控制＿＿＿＿＿＿＿＿。
gōngsī bìxū kǒngzhì

人员流动
rényuán liúdòng

people flow

招待费用
zhāodài fèiyòng

reception fees

办公支出
bàngōng zhīchū

office expenditure

Production costs are the costs for the production of products, it includes material the products are made of, power, salary and welfare of the production staff, manufacture fees and others.

57

公司每年要上交一定的所得税。

Gōngsī měi nián yào shàngjiāo yídìng de suǒdéshuì.

The company turns in a certain amount of income tax each year.

每年要交哪些税？

Měi nián yào jiāo nǎxiē shuì?

公司每年要上交一定的

Gōngsī měi nián yào shàngjiāo yídìng de

所得税，还有其他的税款。

suǒdéshuì, háiyǒu qítā de shuìkuǎn.

What taxes should be paid each year?

The company turns in a certain amount of income tax each year. There are other taxes.

公司每年要上交一定的_____。
gōngsī měi nián yào shàngjiāo yídìng de

营业税
yíngyèshuì

sales tax

增值税
zēngzhíshuì

value added tax

NOTES

Enterprise income tax rates are divided into three levels: 18%, 27% and 33%. We can see from the profit table that profit of the year × tax rate = due income tax. For those enterprises whose annual taxable income is lower than RMB 30,000 (inclusive), an 18% tax rate is applied for the collection of its income tax. For those enterprises whose annual taxable income is between RMB 100,000 (inclusive) and RMB 30,000, a 27% tax rate is applied. For those enterprises whose annual taxable income is above RMB 100,000, an 33% tax rate is applied.

58

德勤是一家知名的会计师事务所。

Déqín shì yì jiā zhīmíng de kuàijìshī shìwùsuǒ.

Deloitte Touche Tohmatsu is a renowned CPAs office.

● 你知道德勤吗？

Nǐ zhīdào Déqín ma?

● 知道，德勤是一家知名的

Zhīdào, Déqín shì yì jiā zhīmíng de

会计师事务所。

kuàijìshī shìwùsuǒ.

● Do you happen to know Deloitte Touche Tohmatsu?

● Yes, I do. Deloitte Touche Tohmatsu is a renowned CPAs office.

_____是一家知名的_____。
shì yì jiā zhīmíng de

毕马威／会计师事务所
Bìmǎwēi ／ kuàijìshī shìwùsuǒ

KPMG/CPAs office

普华永道／审计公司
Pǔhuá Yǒngdáo／ shěnjì gōngsī

PricewaterhouseCoopers/audit office

新浪／新闻网站
Xīnlàng ／ xīnwén wǎngzhàn

Sina/news website

NOTES

Deloitte, Ernst & Young, KPMG and PricewaterhouseCooper are the four major renowned CPAs offices in the world. Since 1980s, Deloitte has opened new offices, and has 5000 employees in Hong Kong, Macao and the Chinese Mainland, including Beijing, Dalian, Guangzhou, Nanjing, Shanghai, Shenzhen, Suzhou and Tianjin.

59

他们完成了今年的财务报表。

Tāmen wánchéng le jīnnián de cáiwù bāobiǎo.

They have finished this year's financial report.

- 财务报表做完了吗？
  Cáiwù bāobiǎo zuò wán le ma?

- 他们刚刚完成了今年的财务
  Tāmen gānggāng wánchéng le jīnnián de cáiwù
  报表。
  bāobiǎo.

- Is the financial report ready now?
- They have just finished this year's financial report.

他们完成了今年的 _____。
tāmen wánchéng le jīnnián de

财务预算
cáiwù yùsuàn
financial budget

审计
shěnjì
audit

工作总结
gōngzuǒ zǒngjié
working summary

NOTES

The financial report of a listed company reflects comprehensively the financial situation, business performance and development trend of a company. It is the most comprehensive, detailed, and often the most reliable first-hand material for investors to understand the company and make decisions on their investment accordingly.

60

上市公司每年都要进行财务审计。

Shàngshì gōngsī měi nián dōu yào jìnxíng cáiwù shěnjì.

Listed companies are required to conduct a financial audit each year.

● 公司上市后需要公开财务吗？

Gōngsī shàngshì hòu xūyào gōngkāi cáiwù ma?

● 是的，上市公司每年都要

Shì de, shàngshì gōngsī měi nián dōu yào

进行财务审计。

jìnxíng cáiwù shěnjì.

● Does the company have to publicize its financial statements after it is listed?

● Yes, listed companies are required to conduct a financial audit each year.

上市公司每年都要＿＿＿＿＿＿。
shàngshì gōngsī měi nián dōu yào

公开财务信息
gōngkāi cáiwù xìnxī

publicize the financial information

报告经营情况
bàogào jīngyíng qíngkuàng

report its operation

In Chinese, the word "Shen Ji" (Audit) first appeared in The History of the Song Dynasty (AD 960-1279). Its original meaning, "Shen" meant to examine, while "Ji" meant statement of accounts. And literary, "Shen Ji" meant examining the statement of accounts. The English word for "Shen Ji" is "audit", which is denoted as "an examination of records or financial accounts", and "to attend to something". Thus, we can see that earlier auditing simply meant the examination of accountants' records.

61

上海是中国的经济和金融中心。
Shànghǎi shì Zhōngguó de jīngjì hé jīnróng zhōngxīn.

Shanghai is China's economic and financial center.

● 北京是中国的政治中心，
　Běijīng shì Zhōngguó de zhèngzhì zhōngxīn,
那么上海呢？
náme Shànghǎi ne?

● 上海是中国的经济和金融
　Shànghǎi shì Zhōngguó de jīngjì hé jīnróng
中心。
zhōngxīn.

● Beijing is China's political center. What about Shanghai?
● Shanghai is China's economic and financial center.

_____是 _____的 _____中心。
　　　shì　　　　de　　　　　zhōngxīn

纽约 / 美国 / 金融
Niǔyuē / Měiguó / jīnróng

香港／亚洲／贸易
Xiānggǎng /Yàzhōu / màoyì

巴黎／法国／文化
Bālí / Fǎguó / wénhuà

NOTES

As an important city in China's reform and opening up, Shanghai has seen a rapid development in its economy and prosperity and stability in society. In 2005, Shanghai has basically established its status as a market-oriented domestic financial center. It is now making headways towards building an international financial center. By the end of 2005, there are altogether 123 foreign-funded operational financial institutions in Shanghai, among which 14 are entitled to operate RMB business.

Securities Market ◎ 证券市场

62

现在我该买进股票还是基金?

Xiànzài wǒ gāi mǎijìn gǔpiào háishi jījīn?

Should I buy stocks or funds now?

○ 现在我该买进股票还是基金?
Xiànzài wǒ gāi mǎijìn gǔpiào háishi jījīn?

● 基金的收益比较好，我建议
Jījīn de shōuyì bǐjiào hǎo, wǒ jiànyì

你买基金。
nǐ mǎi jījīn.

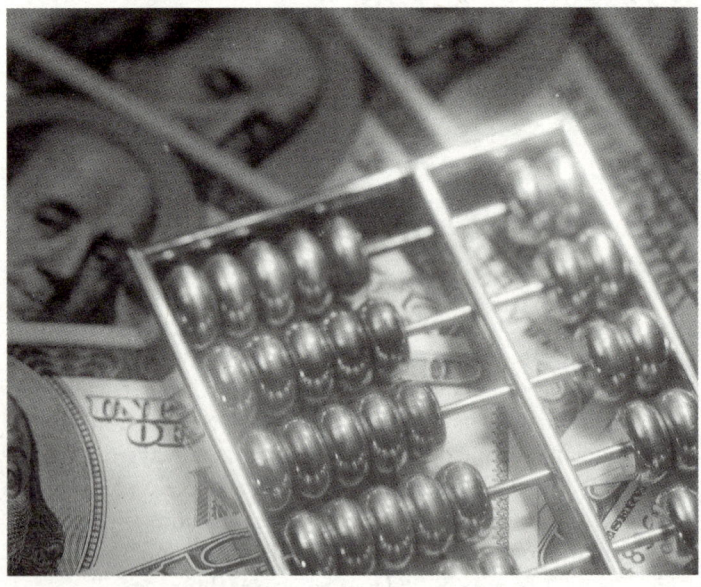

○ Should I buy stocks or funds now?
● Funds were better proceeds. I suggest you buy a fund.

现在我该买进股票还是＿＿＿？
xiànzài wǒ gāi mǎijìn gǔpiào háishi

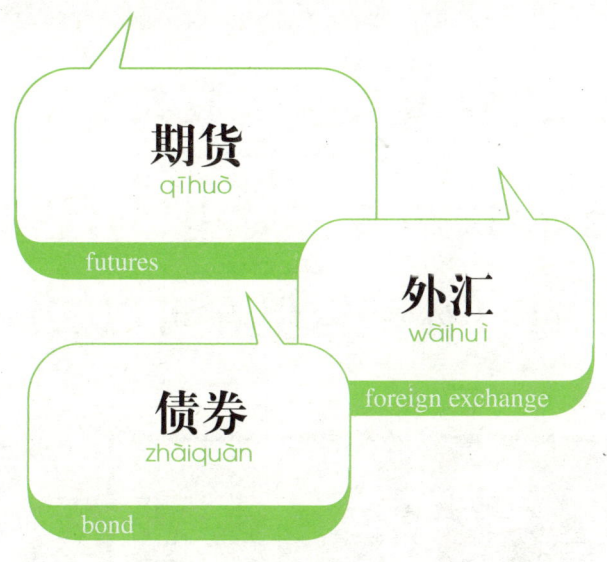

期货
qīhuò

futures

外汇
wàihuì

foreign exchange

债券
zhàiquàn

bond

NOTES

Buying a fund means an investor is entrusting a fund management company to engage in investments in stocks and bonds, while buying stocks means that he becomes the stockholder of a listed company. Funds usually invest in many stocks, and will thus effectively distribute relevant risks and result in more stable yields. A unitary investment in a certain stock usually can not effectively distributes relevant risks. In return, its yield will face larger risks and will be more fluctuating.

63

在这些蓝筹股中，GE 上涨了 1%。

Zài zhèxiē lánchóugǔ zhōng, GE shàngzhǎng le bǎifēnzhīyī.

Among all blue chips, GE has increased by 1%.

● 我 应该 买 哪 只 股票？
Wǒ yīnggāi mǎi nǎ zhī gǔpiào?

● 在 这些 蓝筹股 中， GE 上涨
Zài zhèxiē lánchóugǔ zhōng, GE shàng zhǎng

了 1%， 你 现在 可以 买 一些。
le bǎifēnzhīyī, nǐ xiànzài kěyǐ mǎi yìxiē.

● Which share should I buy?
● Among all blue chips, GE has increased by 1%. You might buy some of it.

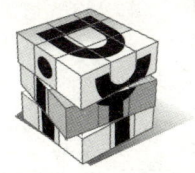

在这些＿＿＿＿中，＿＿＿＿
zài zhèxiē   zhōng
上涨了 1%。
shàngzhǎng le bǎifēnzhīyī

绩优股 / 中石化
jìyōugǔ / Zhōngshíhuà

blue chip/Sinochem

普通股 / 海尔
pǔtōng gǔ / Hǎi'ěr

ordinary share /Haier

红 筹 股 / 国美
hóngchóugǔ / Guóměi

red chips/Gome

NOTES

Blue chips refer to large-scale, traditional industrial shares with long-term stable increase and financial shares. Listed companies issuing such shares have excellent business performance, stable yields, large scale capitalization, good dividends, stable in the share price momentum, and a good market image.

64

成长型企业融资比较容易。

Chéngzhǎngxíng qǐyè róngzī bǐjiào róngyì.

It is easier for emerging enterprises to get financing.

● 哪种企业融资比较容易？

Nǎ zhǒng qǐyè róngzī bǐjiào róngyì?

● 成长型企业融资比较容易。

Chéngzhǎngxíng qǐyè róngzī bǐjiào róngyì.

○ Which enterprises can get financing more easily?

● It is easier for emerging enterprises to get financing.

_____企业 _____比较容易。
　　　　qǐyè　　　　　　　bǐjiào róngyì

国有 / 贷款
guóyǒu / dàikuǎn

state-own/loans

小型 / 转型
xiǎoxíng / zhuǎnxíng

small/transform

电信 / 获利
diànxìn / huòlì

telecommunication/
make benefits

Financing could be divided into direct and indirect financing. Direct financing does not go through financial institutions, rather, it is the financing activity conducted by governments, enterprises, organizations and individuals, in the capacity of a final borrower, on the final loan supplier. The resulted finance will be used in production, investment and consumption. While indirect financing is the financing conducted by the final borrower on the final loan supplier through the agent of financial institutions, e.g., enterprises' financing from banks, trust company, etc....

65

公司的股票是在 5 年前挂牌上市的。

Gōngsī de gǔpiào shì zài wǔ nián qián guàpái shàngshì de.

The share of the company was listed five years ago.

● 公司的股票上市多久了？

　　Gōngsī de gǔpiào shàngshì duō jiǔ le?

● 公司的股票是在 5 年前挂牌

　　Gōngsī de gǔpiào shì zài wǔ niánqián guàpái

上市的。

shàngshì de.

○ How long have the shares of the company been listed?

● The share of the company was listed five years ago.

公司的股票是在 5 年前＿＿＿
gōngsī de gǔpiào shì zài wǔ niánqián
上市的。
shàngshì de

申请
shēnqǐng

applied

在二板市场
zài èrbǎn shìchǎng

on the second-board market

在香港股市
zài xiānggǎng gǔshì

in Hong Kong security market

NOTES

After shares come into the market, listed companies will then become the investment targets of mass investors. Thus it will be easier to attract their savings and fund, enlarging the companies resources of financing preparation. The direct effect of the decentralization of its shares and popularization of capitals of the listed company is the enormous increase of shareholders, who will in turn, buy the products of the company for themselves and their friends and relatives alike.

66

公司去年12月发行了2000万股股票。

Gōngsī qùnián shí'èr yuè fāxíng le liǎngqiān wàn gǔ gǔpiào.

The company issued 20 million shares last December.

● 公司发行股票了吗？

Gōngsī fāxíng gǔpiào le ma?

● 公司去年 12 月发行了 2000

Gōngsī qùnián shí'èr yuè fāxíng le liǎngqiān

万股股票。

wàn gǔ gǔpiào.

● Has the company issued any shares?
● The company issued 20 million shares last December.

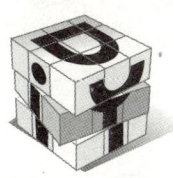

公司 去 年 12 月 _____ 了
gōngsī qùnián shí'èr yuè le

2000 万 股 股票。
liǎngqiān wǎn gǔ gǔpiào

增发
zēngfā

added

派发
pàifā

sent out

送出
sòngchū

delivered

NOTES

When shares come into the market, the listed companies will take into account their own interests and try to ensure a successful launch of their shares. To achieve that, they will not issue these shares by their face value, but rather, issue at a more reasonable price, which is called the offering price. A bargain price will be set in trading, which is usually called market price of the shares. Market prices of any shares change constantly, as they are affected by a throng of factors.

67

政府将在下个星期发行新的国债。

Zhèngfǔ jiāng zài xià gè xīngqī fāxíng xīn de guózhài.

The government will issue new national debt next week.

● 新的国债什么时候发行？

Xīn de guózhài shénme shíhou fāxíng?

● 政府将在下个星期发行新

Zhèngfǔ jiāng zài xià gè xīngqī fāxíng xīn

的国债。

de guózhài.

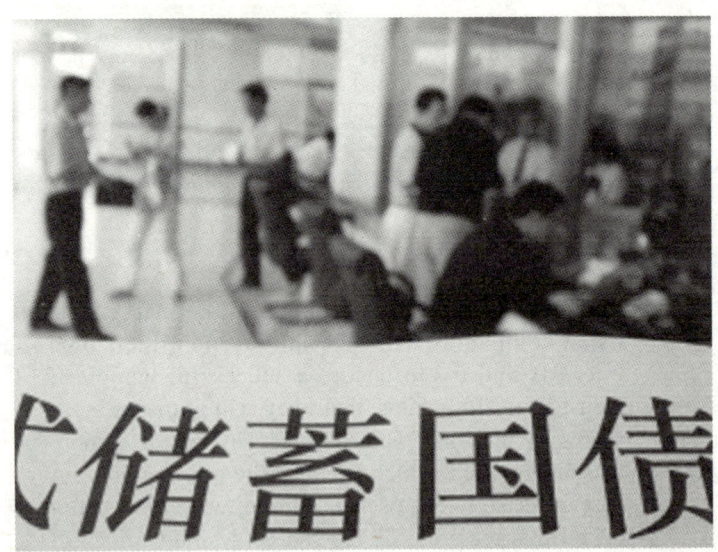

● When will the government issue the new national debt?
● The government will issue new national debt next week.

政府将在下个星期发行新的
zhèngfǔ jiāng zài xià gè xīngqī fāxíng xīn de

_____ 。

地方债券
dìfāng zhàiquàn

local debt

普通债券
pǔtōng zhàiquàn

common debt

可转换债券
kězhuǎnhuàn zhàiquàn

convertible debt

> **NOTES**
>
> National debt are bonds issued by a government. Compared with other types of bonds, the subject of the national debt is the state which possesses an extremely high credibility. National debt is indirectly issued through securities operation institution, and investors can purchase national debt in such institutions.

68

石油期货的价格每天都有变化。

Shíyóu qīhuò de jiàgé měitiān dōu yǒu biànhuà.

There is a change everyday in the price of petroleum futures.

● 石油期货的风险大吗？

Shíyóu qīhuò de fēngxiǎn dà ma?

● 相当 大，特别是最近，石油

Xiāngdāng dà, tèbié shì zuìjìn, shíyóu

期货的价格每天都有变化。

qīhuò de jiàgé měitiān dōu yǒu biànhuà.

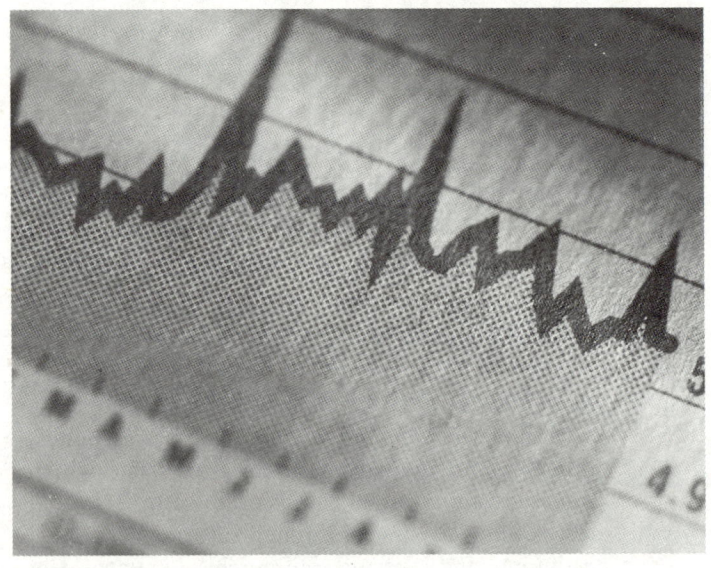

○ Are there high risks for petroleum futures?

● Rather high. There is a change everyday in the price of petroleum futures, especially recently.

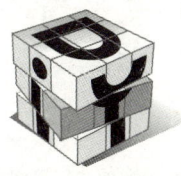

期货的价格
qīhuò de jiàgé

每天都有变化。
měitiān dōu yǒu biànhuà

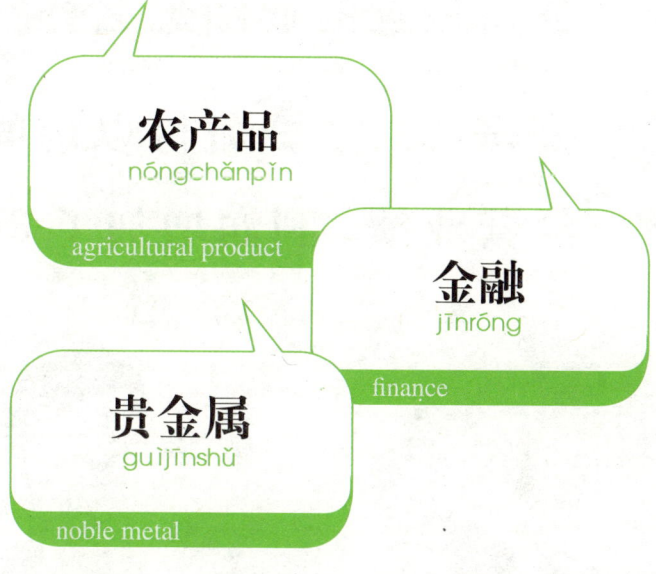

农产品
nóngchǎnpǐn

agricultural product

金融
jīnróng

finance

贵金属
guìjīnshǔ

noble metal

NOTES

Futures are contracted trade, i.e., mutual transaction of contracts. There is a day of contango for the completion of futures transaction. Before that contango day, it is contract trade; while after that, spot transactions are needed to fulfill the contract. Futures covers only limited categories, mainly agriculture, petroleum, metal commodities and other preliminary raw material and financial products.

69

公司公布了9月份以前的经营业绩，利润增加了30%。

Gōngsī gōngbù le jiǔ yuèfèn yǐqián de jīngyíng yèjì, lìrùn zēngjiā le bǎifēnzhīsānshí.

The company publicized their business performance before September; its profit has increased by 30%.

● 公司最近的业绩怎么样？

Gōngsī zuìjìn de yèjì zěnmeyàng?

● 公司公布了9月份以前的

Gōngsī gōngbù le jiǔ yuèfèn yǐqián de

经营业绩，利润增加了30%。

jīngyíng yèjì, lìrùn zēngjiā le bǎifēnzhīsānshí.

● How was the company's recent performance?

● The company has publicized the business performance before September; its profit has increased by 30%.

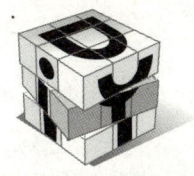

公司＿＿＿＿＿了9月份以前的
gōngsī　　　　　　le jiǔ yuèfèn yǐqián de

经营业绩，利润增加了30%。
jīngyíng yèjì　lìrùn zēngjiā le bǎifēnzhīsānshí

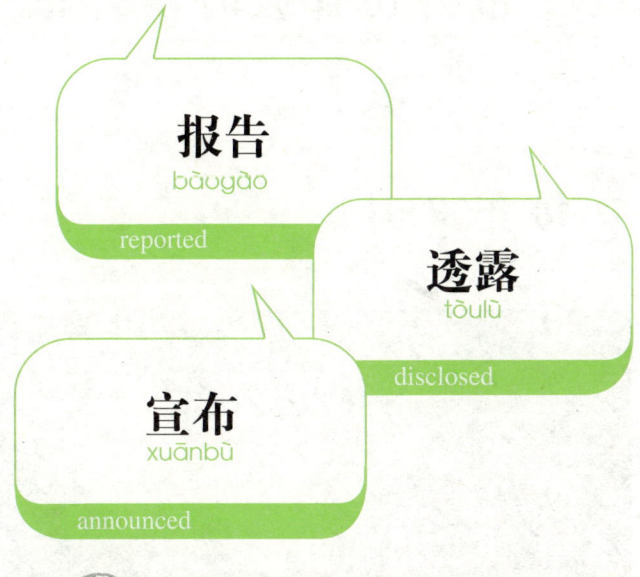

报告
bàogào

reported

透露
tòulù

disclosed

宣布
xuānbù

announced

Affected by various factors, e.g., the business performance of the enterprise issuing the stock, the price of a stock will change. If the enterprise is well managed and is making abundant profit, then its shares' price and quotation will increase. Otherwise, the value and price of the share will decrease, or even no one will buy it, as a result, its prospect will look deem.

70

上市公司什么时候公布年度财务报表?
Shàngshì gōngsī shénme shíhou gōngbù niándù cáiwù bàobiǎo?

When do listed companies publicize their financial reports?

● 上市公司什么时候公布年度
Shàngshì gōngsī shénme shíhou gōngbù niándù

财务报表?
cáiwù bàobiǎo?

● 每年3月。
Měinián sān yuè.

● When do listed companies publicize their financial reports?
● Every March.

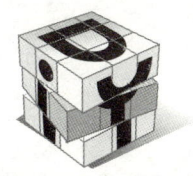

上市公司什么时候公布
shàngshì gōngsī shénme shíhou gōngbù

_____ ?

经营状况
jīngyíng zhuàngkuàng

business performance

盈利情况
yínglì qíngkuàng

profit situation

业绩报告
yèjì bàogào

business performance report

Founded on April 8, 1987, China Merchants Bank is the first share-holding commercial bank wholly owned by corporate legal entities. Since its establishment, the bank has undergone capital enlargement by 3 times, and launched IPO with the issuance of 1.5 billion common shares in March 2002. By the end of 2006, the total asset of China Merchants Bank is above 800 billion Yuan (RMB), and is ranked the top 114 among "the world 1000 banks" by British financial journal *The Banker*.

71

评估结果已经反馈给了人力资源部。

Pínggū jiéguǒ yǐjīng fǎnkuì gěi le rénlì zīyuánbù.

The assessment results have been forwarded to the Human Resource Department.

● 评估结果交给哪个部门了？

Pínggū jiéguǒ jiāogěi nǎge bùmén le?

● 评估结果已经反馈给了人力资源部。

Pínggū jiéguǒ yǐjīng fǎnkuì gěi le rénlì zīyuánbù.

人力资源部

● Which department have the assessment results been forwarded to?

● The assessment results have been forwarded to the Human Resource Department.

_____已经反馈给了人力
　　　　　yǐjīng fǎnkuì gěi le rénlì

资源部。
zīyuánbù

调查结果
diàochá jiéguǒ

investigation results

员工意见
yuángōng yìjiàn

employees' opinion

考核成绩
kǎohé chéngjì

test results

NOTES

Many companies regularly assess their employees' performance by using a method of performance management. They link the employee's salary, professional development opportunities, welfare and bonus with his work performance, thus encouraging the employees to do a better job.

72

我们分析了最近三个月的市场销售情况。

Wǒmen fēnxī le zuìjìn sān gè yuè de shìchǎng xiāoshòu qíngkuàng.

We have analyzed the selling situation in the recent three months.

● 我们分析了最近三个月的

Wǒmen fēnxī le zuìjìn sān gè yuè de

市场销售情况。

shìchǎng xiāoshòu qíngkuàng.

● 你们得出了什么结论？

Nǐmen déchū le shénme jiélùn?

● We have analyzed the selling situation in the recent three months.

● What conclusion have you drawn?

我们分析了最近三个月的

wǒmen   fēnxī   le   zuìjìn   sān   gè   yuè   de

_____。

流行趋势
liúxíng   qūshì

fashion trend

消费者需求
xiāofèizhě   xūqiú

consumer demands

购买趋势
gǒumǎi   qūshì

purchase tendency

In the 21st century, consumption products have entered a scenario where supply exceeds demand. Both manufacturers and dealers have to understand consumers' demand constantly, and supply diversified products for the market. After launching a certain product, they have to trace down the change of the market constantly, so that they might maintain their leadership in that certain industry.

73

你参加公司周三的例会吗？

Nǐ   cānjiā   gōngsī   zhōu sān   de   lìhuì   ma?

Will you attend the company's regular meeting on Wednesday?

● 你参加公司周三的例会吗？

Nǐ   cānjiā   gōngsī   zhōu sān   de   lìhuì   ma?

● 这周不行，我明天出差。

Zhè zhōu bù xíng,   wǒ míngtiān chūchāi.

● Will you attend the company's regular meeting on Wednesday?

● Not this week. I am going on a business trip tomorrow.

你参加公司周三的_____吗？
nǐ cānjiā gōngsī zhōusān de ma

研讨会
yántǎo huì

workshop

产品发布会
chǎnpǐn fābùhuì

new product release

展销会
zhǎnxiāohuì

exhibition and selling fair

NOTES

For many high and middle managers, attending the regular meeting in their companies is a good opportunity for communication. They can get to know whether their colleagues are cooperating in terms of work process; they can enhance their efficiency in work, strengthen the teamwork spirit, so as to implement their companies' general objectives of common development.

74

网络广告的效果怎么样?

Wǎngluò guǎnggào de xiǎoguǒ zěnmeyàng?

What were the effects of the Internet advertisements?

● 网络广告的效果怎么样?

Wǎngluòguǎnggàode xiǎoguǒ zěnmeyàng?

● 效果很好,有很多公司给

Xiǎoguǒ hěn hǎo, yǒu hěnduō gōngsī gěi

我们下了订单。

wǒmen xià le dìngdān.

● What were the effects of the Internet advertisements?
● Very good. Many companies have given their orders to us.

网络广告的_____怎么样？
wǎngluò guǎnggào de _____ zěnmeyàng

点击率
diǎnjīlǜ
click through rate

收入
shōurù
earning

费用
fèiyòng
cost

Internet advertisements are featured with low prices and good effect. If the target customers of a certain product are young people, using Internet advertisement will usually be useful. When people are selling cell phones, computer software, western fast food, drinks and the like, people will include Internet as one of the advertisement medium.

75

您希望售后服务有哪方面的改进?

Nín xīwàng shòuhòu fúwù yǒu nǎ fāngmiàn de gǎijìn?

What improvements do you expect from our after service?

- 您希望**售后服务**有哪方面的
  Nín xīwàng shòuhòu fúwù yǒu nǎ fāngmiàn de

  改进？
  gǎijìn?

- 我希望能开通800免费客户
  Wǒ xīwàng néng kāitōng bālínglíng miǎnfèi kèhù

  服务热线。
  fúwù rèxiàn.

- What improvements do you hope from our after service?
- I hope an 800 free customer service hotline will be opened.

您希望_____有哪方面的改进？
nín xīwǎng　　　　　yǒu nǎ fāngmiàn de　gǎijìn

产品质量
chǎnpǐn zhìliàng

quality of the products

产品设计
chǎnpǐn shèjì

design of the products

产品包装
chǎnpǐn bāozhuāng

packing of the products

NOTES

　　After-service is now attracting more and more emphasis from enterprises. Providing fast, convenient and good-quality after-service embodies the respect towards customers, so that customers can be confident in the products they bought. Thus cultivating some favor for both the manufacturers and the dealers, which helps maintain good reputation of the company. Also , profit resulting from after-service could not be neglected, either.

151

76

经理每天花大量的时间与员工进行沟通。

Jīnglǐ měitiān huā dàliàng de shíjiān yǔ yuángōng jìnxíng gōutōng.

The manager spends a lot of time communicating with his staff every day.

● 经理与员工沟通的时间多
Jīnglǐ yǔ yuángōng gōutōng de shíjiān duō
吗?
ma?

● 经理每天花大量的时间与
Jīnglǐ měitiān huā dàliàng de shíjiān yǔ
员工进行沟通。
yuángōng jìnxíng gōutōng.

● Do the managers spend time communicating with their staff?
● The manager spends a lot of time communicating with his staff every day.

经理每天花大量的时间
jīnglǐ měitiān huā dàliàng de shíjiān

_____。

拜访客户
bǎifǎng kèhù

visiting his customer

批示文件
pīshì wénjiàn

giving remarks on documents

参加会议
cānjiā huìyì

attending meetings

NOTES

A professional manager must spend much of his time and energy to solving communication problems. When he is about to have a face-to-face talk with internal people, the following three points are least requirements: arriving on time; calculating in advance how much time will be needed for the meeting; and, proposing the meeting topics.

Information Management ◎ 信息管理

153

77

公司秘书每天都要回复信件、传真和电子邮件。
Gōngsī mìshū měitiān dōuyào huífù xìnjiàn, chuánzhēn hé diànzǐ yóujiàn.

A secretary of a company has to reply to letters, faxes and emails every day.

秘书的日常工作有哪些？
Mìshū de rìcháng gōngzuò yǒu nǎxiē?

公司秘书每天都要回复
Gōngsī mìshū měitiān dōuyào huífù

信件、传真和电子邮件。
xìnjiàn, chuánzhēn hé diànzǐ yóujiàn.

What is the daily work of a secretary?

A secretary of a company has to reply letters, faxes and emails every day.

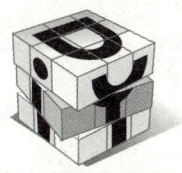

公司秘书每天都要＿＿＿＿＿
gōngsī mìshū měitiān dōuyào
信件、传真和电子邮件。
xìnjiàn   chuánzhēn hé diànzǐ yóujiàn

发送
fāsòng

send

接收
jiēshōu

receive

整理
zhěnglǐ

arrange

NOTES

According to statistics, there are about 23 million people in China engaging in secretarial work. They become increasingly executive assistants participating in corporate management. They not only have to master the working skills in the office, but also have to display responsibility when left unattended by their supervisors. They should also take initiative and make judgment and prompt decisions with the authority they are given.

78

电子邮件是人们常用的非正式的沟通方式。

Diànzǐ yóujiàn shì rénmen chángyòng de fēizhèngshì de gōutōng fāngshì.

Email is an informal communication means often used.

● 人们现在习惯用什么方式
Rénmen xiànzài xíguàn yòng shénme fāngshì

沟通？
gōutōng?

● 电子邮件是人们常用的
Diànzǐ yóujiàn shì rénmen chángyòng de

非正式的沟通方式。
fēizhèngshì de gōutōng fāngshì.

● What communication means do people usually employ nowadays?

● Email is an informal communication means often used.

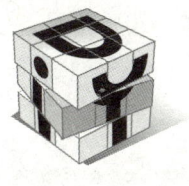

_____是人们常用的_____
shì rénmen chángyòng de

的沟通方式。
de gōutōng fāngshì

MSN／非正式
M S N ／ fēizhèngshì

全体员工大会
quántǐ yuángōng dàhuì
／正式
／ zhèngshì

书面报告 ／ 正式
shūmiàn bǎogào ／ zhèngshì

NOTES

Informal communication is one conducted with employees in informal occasions; commonly used means of communication may include email, net chatting by chat programs or having dinner or tea together. The company might also hold entertainment activities, in which both supervisors and employees may attend. That way it will help foster closer ties with employees and better understanding about them.

79

海外市场的负责人经常要和总部沟通。

Hǎiwài shìchǎng de fùzérén jīngcháng yào hé zǒngbù gōutōng.

People in charge of overseas markets must communicate with headquarters.

● 总部如何了解海外公司的
Zǒngbù rúhé liǎojiě hǎiwài gōngsī de
情况？
qíngkuàng?

● 海外市场的负责人经常要
Hǎiwài shìchǎng de fùzérén jīngcháng yào
和总部沟通。
hé zǒngbù gōutōng.

● How does the headquarters learn about the situation of
its overseas companies?

● People in charge of overseas markets must communicate
with headquarters.

海外市场的负责人经常要和
hǎiwài shìchǎng de fùzérén jīngcháng yào hé

＿＿＿＿＿＿沟通。
gōutōng

地区负责人
dìqū fùzérén

people in charge of a district

当地有关部门
dāngdì yǒuguān bùmén

local departments

合作伙伴
hézuò huǒbàn

cooperation partners

NOTES

The company or the product image of a multinational company is globally unified, but the company has to take into account the specialty of the overseas markets at the same time. It is one of the essential jobs for people in charge of overseas markets to maintain frequent communication with headquarters.

80

企业信息管理师从事信息资源的开发和利用工作。
Qǐyè xìnxī guǎnlǐshī cóngshì xìnxī zīyuán de kāifā hé lìyòng gōngzuò.

The manager for enterprise information engages in the development and utilization of information resources.

● 企业信息管理师的职责是
　Qǐyè xìnxī guǎnlǐshī de zhízé shì

什么呢？
shénme ne?

● 企业信息管理师从事信息
　Qǐyè xìnxī guǎnlǐshī cóngshì xìnxī

资源的开发和利用工作。
zīyuán de kāifā hé lìyòng gōngzuò.

● What is the responsibility of the manager for enterprise information?

● The manager for enterprise information engages in the development and utilization of information resources.

企 业 信 息 管 理 师 从 事 信 息 资 源
qǐyè   xìnxī   guǎnlǐshī   cóngshì   xìnxī   zīyuán

的 ＿＿＿＿＿和 利 用 工 作 。
de   hé   lìyòng   gōngzuò

建设
jiànshè

construction

管理
guǎnlǐ

management

整合
zhěnghé

integration

Management conceptions of Chinese enterprises must change after China's entry in WTO. They must materialize management modernization, taking information development as the core, so as to enhance their competitiveness in the market. Under the above circumstance, China formulated and promulgated the State Professional Standard for Managers in Enterprise Information. Managers in Enterprise Information engage in the construction of enterprise information, and are responsible for the IT application, development, maintenance and management of information systems, and the development and utilization of information resources.

81

年轻人喜欢用信用卡消费，老年人还是习惯用现金。
Nniánqīngrén xǐhuan yòng xìnyòngkǎ xiāofèi, lǎoniánrén háishi xíguàn yòng xiànjīn.

While young men like to use credit cards, the elders are used to cash.

● 现 在 用 信 用 卡 的 中 国 人 多
Xiànzài yòng xìnyòng kǎ de Zhōngguórén duō

不 多 ?
bù duō?

● 越 来 越 多 的 年 轻 人 喜 欢 用
Yuèláiyuèduō de niánqīng rén xǐhuan yòng

信 用 卡 消 费 ， 不 过 老 年 人
xìnyòngkǎ xiāofèi, búguò lǎonián rén

还 是 习 惯 用 现 金 。
háishi xíguàn yòng xiànjīn.

● Do many Chinese use credit cards in China now?

● More and more young men like to use credit cards.
However, the elders are used to cash.

年轻人喜欢用_____消费，
niánqīngrén　xǐhuan yǒng　　　　　　xiāofèi,

老年人还是习惯用现金。
lǎoniánrén　háishi　xíguàn yǒng xiànjīn

支票
zhīpiào

cheque

远程支付方式
yuǎnchéng zhīfù fāngshì

telepayment means

银行卡
yínhángkǎ

bank cards

In recent years, holders of credit cards of different banks are enjoying more and more convenience and safer services, including the double-currency or multi-currency card, global accepting card, perfect safeguard card against card losses, 24-hour global emergency assistance card, and cards which offer special discounts for holders or lends cash to holders.

82

我可以采用分期付款的方式吗?

Wǒ kěyǐ cǎiyòng fēnqī fùkuǎn de fāngshì ma?

May I take the form of a divided payment?

● 我 可 以 采 用 分 期 付 款 的 方 式
Wǒ kěyǐ cǎiyòng fēnqī fùkuǎn de fāngshì

吗?
ma?

● 如 果 您 的 消 费 满 千 元 以 上,
Rúguǒ nín de xiāofèi mǎn qiān yuán yǐ shàng,

可 以 分 期 付 款。
kěyǐ fēnqī fùkuǎn.

● May I take the form of a divided payment?
● You may if your consumption exceeds 1000 RMB.

我可以采用＿＿＿＿的方式吗？
wǒ kěyǐ cǎiyòng   de fāngshì ma

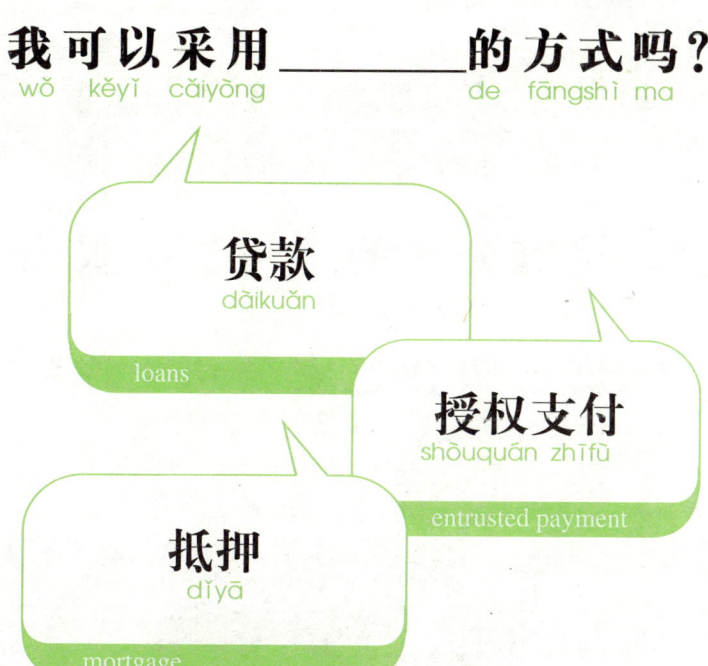

贷款
dàikuǎn

loans

授权支付
shòuquán zhīfù

entrusted payment

抵押
dǐyā

mortgage

NOTES

One may divide the total price into several factions and pay it on a monthly basis when one is purchasing certain goods. Divided payment is the agreement that a bank has with a shop owner, and the shop owners could require that with credit cards from certain banks that offer divided payments. In this circumstance, the credit limit will be deducted to the same amount as the total price of the commodity. The consumers pay monthly installments to their own credit cards, as prompt return of payment will prevent interest fees from emerging.

83

这家公司的信用等级很高。

Zhè jiā gōngsī de xìnyòng děngjí hěn gāo.

The credit rating of this company is rather high.

- 这家公司的信用等级很高。
  Zhè jiā gōngsī de xìnyòng děngjí hěn gāo.

- 真希望在这家公司工作啊！
  Zhēn xīwàng zài zhè jiā gōngsī gōngzuò a!

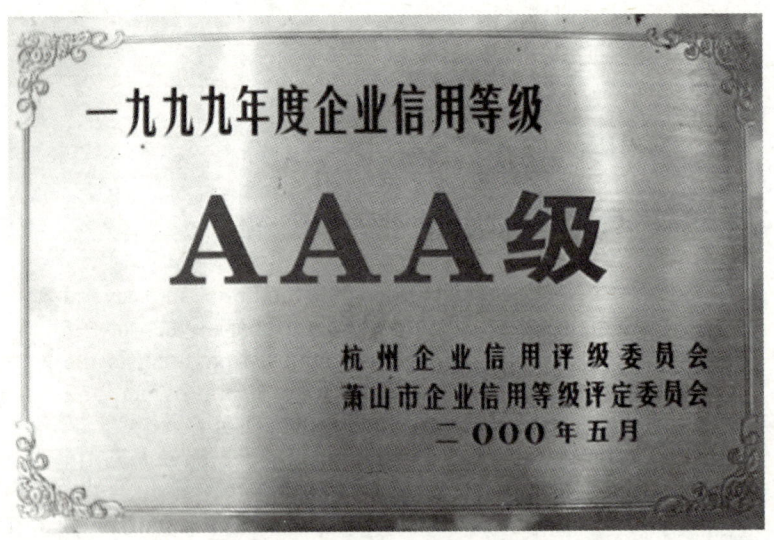

The credit rating of this company is rather high.

How I wish I could work in the company!

这家公司的＿＿＿＿＿很高。
zhè jiā gōngsī de　　　　　　hěn gāo

品牌价值
pǐnpái jiàzhí

brand value

全球知名度
quánqiú zhīmíngdù

global awareness

股票收益
gǔpiào shōuyì

stock yields

Corporate credit includes: corporate credit in organization, in the market and in banks. To hedge risks in loans, banks will assess an enterprise's capitalization and corporate credit capability, and use a specific quantified standard to rate the corporate credit reputation, and decide whether to grant a loan or not. A bank's credit assessment is very inclusive, and is the most important credit assessment of an enterprise.

84

24 小时电话和网上银行业务最受欢迎。

Èrshísì xiǎoshí diànhuà hé wǎng shàng yínháng yèwù zuì shòu huānyíng

The 24-hour telephone banking service and the internet banking service are most welcomed.

● 什么银行业务最受欢迎？

Shénme yínháng yèwù zuì shòu huānyíng?

● 24 小时电话和网上银行

Èrshísì xiǎoshí diànhuà hé wǎng shàng yínháng

业务最受欢迎。

yèwù zuì shòu huānyíng.

● What banking service is most welcomed?

● The 24-hour telephone banking service and the internet banking service are most welcomed.

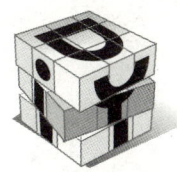

24 小时电话和＿＿＿＿＿
 èrshísì xiǎoshí diànhuà hé

业务最受欢迎。
yèwù zuì shòu huānyíng.

手机钱包
shǒujī qiánbāo

cellphone banking service

电子银行
diànzǐ yínháng

electronic banking service

短信提示
duǎnxìn tíshì

short messages notification

NOTES

Electronic banking service is a general term referring to telephone, internet and cell phone banking service. At present, telephone and internet banking services are widely used. By using telephone and internet banking services, individual and enterprise customers can proceed a series of business including inquiry, transfer, remittance, payment, securities, foreign exchange and fund, without even going to a bank! That way, a more fitting and reliable financial service is offered.

85

商业银行为个人和企业提供贷款。

Shāngyè yínháng wèi gèrén hé qǐyè tígōng dàikuǎn.

Commercial banks provide loans to individuals and enterprises.

- 商业银行为哪些人提供贷款？

  Shāngyè yínháng wèi nǎxiē rén tígōng dàikuǎn?

- 商业银行为个人和企业提供

  Shāngyè yínháng wèi gèrén hé qǐyè tígōng

  贷款。

  dàikuǎn.

- Who do commercial banks provide loans to?
- Commercial banks provide loans to individuals and enterprises.

商业银行为个人和企业提供
shāngyè yínháng wèi gèrén hé qǐyè tígōng

外汇业务
wàihuì yèwù
foreign exchange business

投资服务
tóuzī fúwù
investment service

理财服务
lǐcái fúwù
financing service

NOTES

To borrow a loan from a bank, one must have a long-term and stable income resource capable of paying monthly capital and interests, and a warrantor and warranty. Furthermore, the total amount of the loan and the interests resulted this should not exceed half of the assessment value of the warranty.

86

请在支票上填写日期、收款人和金额。
Qǐng zài zhīpiào shang tiánxiě rìqī, shōukuǎnrén hé jīn'é.

Please fill in the date, payee and money amount.

- 请在支票上填写日期、
  Qǐng zài zhīpiào shang tiánxiě rìqī,
  收款人和金额。
  shōukuǎnrén hé jīn'é.

- 好的。
  Hǎode.

- Please fill in the date, payee and money amount.
- O.K.

172

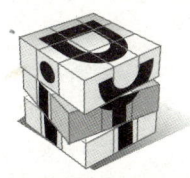

请在_____上填写日期、
qǐng zài shang tiānxiě rìqī,
收款人和金额。
shōukuǎnrén hé jīn'é

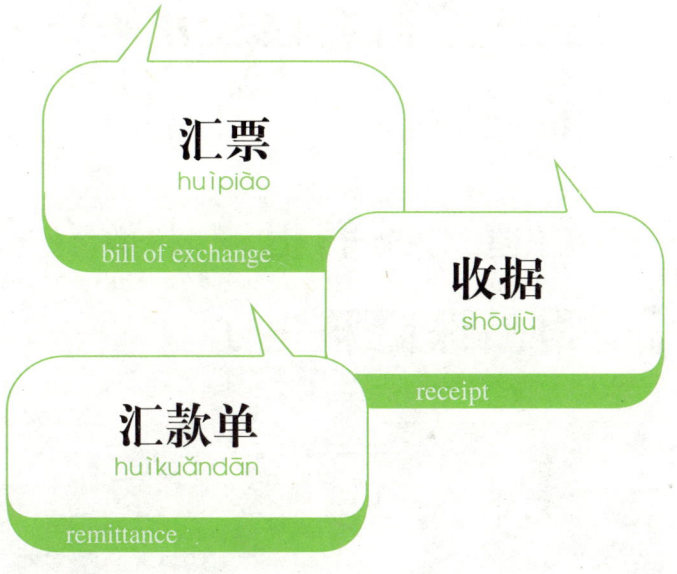

汇票
huìpiào

bill of exchange

收据
shōujù

receipt

汇款单
huìkuǎndān

remittance

Commonly seen cheques include open cheque, cash cheque and cheque for transfer. Cheque clearance is characterized by simplicity, flexibility, fastness and reliability. There should not be any altering marks in the front part of the cheque; otherwise that cheque will become invalid.

87

我们把东西放在贵重物品保险箱里了。

Wǒmen bǎ dōngxī fàng zài guìzhòng wùpǐn bǎoxiǎnxiāng lǐ le.

We have put our things in the safe box.

● 这些东西应该放在一个安全
Zhèxiē dōngxi yīnggāi fàng zài yí gè ānquán

的地方。
de dìfang.

● 知道，我们把东西放在贵重
Zhīdào, wǒmen bǎ dōngxi fàng zài guìzhòng

物品保险箱里了。
wùpǐn bǎoxiǎnxiāng lǐ le.

保管间

● These things should be placed in a safer place.
● O. K. We have put our things in the safe box.

我们把＿＿＿＿＿放在贵重
wǒmen bǎ　　　　　　fàng zài guìzhòng

物品保险箱里了。
wùpǐn bǎoxiǎnxiāng lǐ　le.

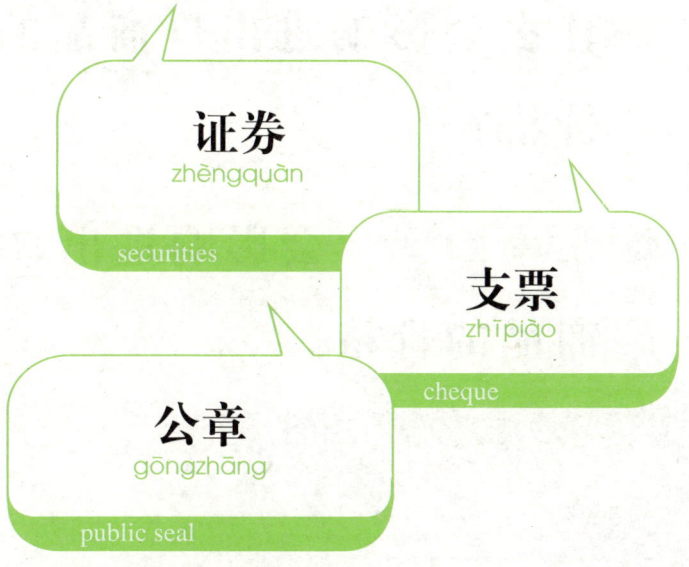

证券
zhèngquàn

securities

支票
zhīpiào

cheque

公章
gōngzhāng

public seal

NOTE:

Security box rental service is a service that a bank opens to keep expensive articles. Renters should be 18 years old or older and must sign a "Box Renting Contract" with a valid ID card to apply for such a rental. The constitution of the fees will include caution money and rental, while the specific amount of money would be decided according to the size of the rented box.

88

汇率的变化会影响进出口商品的价格。

Huìlǜ de biànhuà huì yǐngxiǎng jìnchūkǒu shāngpǐn de jiàgé.

The change of exchange rate will affect the price of the import/export commodities.

● 什么会影响进出口商品的
Shénme huì yǐngxiǎng jìnchūkǒu shāngpǐn de

价格？
jiàgé?

● 汇率的变化会影响进出口
Huìlǜ de biànhuà huì yǐngxiǎng jìnchū kǒu

商品的价格。
shāngpǐn de jiàgé.

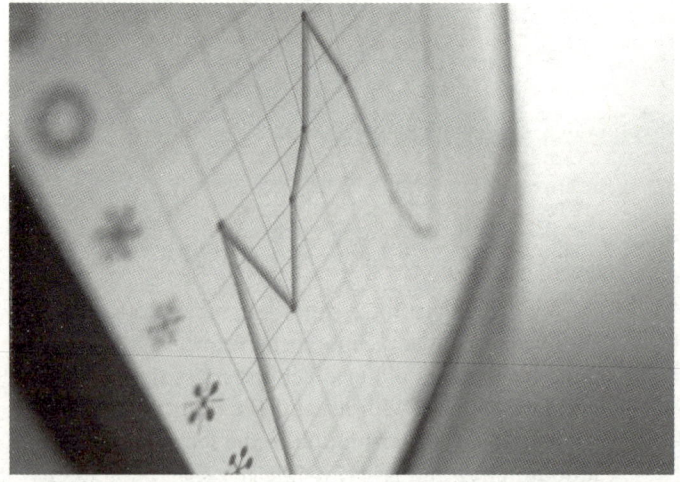

○ What will affect the price of the import/export commodities?

● The change of exchange rate will affect the price of the import/export commodities.

—————————— **会影响进出口**
huì yǐngxiǎng jìnchū kǒu

商品的价格。
shāngpǐn de   jiàgé

支付条件
zhīfù tiáojiàn

Payment conditions

成交量
chéngjiāoliàng

trading volume

相关政策
xiāngguān zhèngcè

relevant policies

NOTES

Exchange rate is a price comparison made between currencies of different countries. The biggest influence that it bring to international trade is that it allows traders to choose one or several stable currencies, i.e., the international currency, like the U.S. $ and EURO€ , as countries back such currencies are capable of making the payment and have a good credit reputation. As a result, using an international currency will also enhance the financial credit of that certain country.

89

请告诉我您的开户银行和开户名。

Qǐng gàosu wǒ nín de kāihù yínháng hé kāihùmíng.

Please tell me your bank and account name.

● 你需要什么信息？

Nǐ xūyào shénme xìnxī?

● 请告诉我您的开户银行和开户名。

Qǐng gàosu wǒ nín de kāihù yínháng hé kāihùmíng.

● What information do you need?

● Please tell me your bank and account name.

请告诉我您的＿＿＿＿＿。
qǐng gàosu wǒ nín de

身份证号码
shēnfènzhèng hàomǎ

ID number

护照号码
hùzhào hàomǎ

number of passports

通讯地址
tōngxùn dìzhǐ

contact address

NOTES

China's banks can be divided approximately into the following categories. 1. The People's Bank of China is the central bank of China; it is in fact an administrative management institution. Basically, it can be said that it is not open to individuals or enterprises. 2. Policy-oriented banks, including the Bank of Agriculture Development and Import/Export Banks, which deal with only policy-related banking services. 3. Commercial banks, in which business is open to enterprises and individuals.

90

他用房子作抵押，向银行贷了 100 万。

Tā yòng fángzi zuò dǐyā, xiāng yínháng dài le yìbǎi wàn.

Mortgaging his house, he borrowed RMB 1 million from a bank.

○ **他怎么筹到钱的？**

Tā zěnme chōu dào qián de?

● **他用房子作抵押，向银行**

Tā yòng fángzi zuò dǐyā, xiāng yínháng

贷了 100 万。

dài le yìbǎi wàn.

○ How did he get the money?

● Mortgaging his house, he borrowed RMB 1 million from a bank.

180

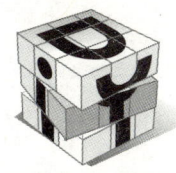

他用＿＿＿＿＿作抵押，向
tā yòng　　　　　　　　zuò dǐyā　xiàng
银行贷了100万。
yínháng dài le　yìbǎi wàn

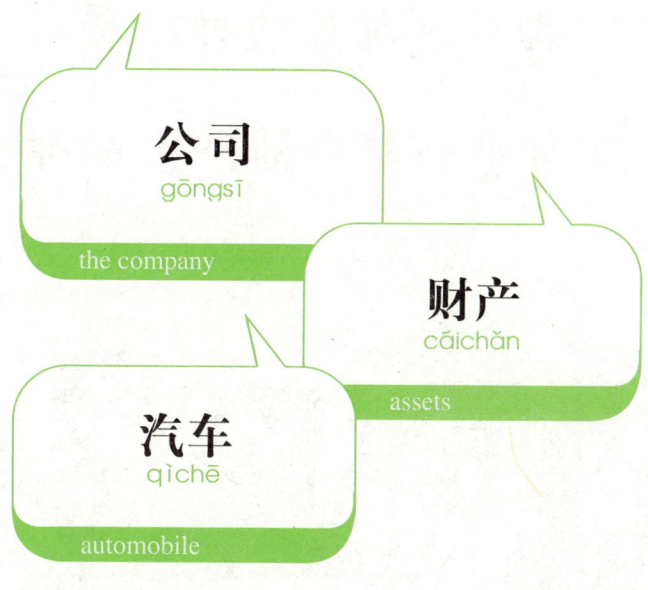

公司
gōngsī

the company

财产
cáichǎn

assets

汽车
qìchē

automobile

The three elements for credit loans are character, capital and capacity. All loans institution will consider these three elements when they are making loan decisions.

91

我看过玩具的样品和目录。
Wǒ kànguò wánjù de yàngpǐn hé mùlù.

I have seen the sample and the toys catalogue.

- 我看过玩具的样品和目录。
  Wǒ kànguò wánjù de yàngpǐn hé mùlù.

- 你准备订购哪些产品呢？
  Nǐ zhǔnbèi dìnggòu nǎxiē chǎnpǐn ne?

- I have seen the sample and the toys catalogue.
- Which products are you going to order?

我看过玩具的样品和＿＿＿＿＿＿＿

wǒ kānguò wánjù de yàngpǐn hé

简介
jiǎnjiè

introduction

报价
bàojià

quoted price

生产过程
shēngchǎn guòchéng

production process

NOTES

It is essential to provide all kinds of quality examination papers when exporting commodities abroad. Take toys as an example, about 75% of the global toys are produced in China. As foreign markets are becoming more and more strict in regard to security standards, Chinese toy exporting companies are developing products meeting environmental protection and security requirements.

92

笔记本电脑的报价是每台600美元，有效期是7天。
Bǐjìběn diànnǎo de bàojià shì měi tái Liùbǎi měiyuán, yǒuxiàoqī shì qī tiān.

Laptop's quotation price is US$600 each, with a period of validity of seven days.

● 笔记本电脑的报价是每台600美元，
Bǐjìběn diànnǎo de bàojià shì měi tái Liùbǎi měiyuán,

有效期是7天。
yǒuxiàoqī shì qī tiān.

● 如果订购的数量大，价格还能再便宜吗？
Rúguǒ dìnggòu de shùliàng dà, jiàgé hái néng zài piányi ma?

● 这个价格不能再低了。
Zhège jiàgé bù néng zài dī le.

● Laptop's quotation price is US$600 each, with a period of validity of seven days.
● Could the price be lower if we order a larger quantity?
● This is the last price.

_____的报价是每台
　　　　　de bàojià shì měi tái

600 美元，有效期是 **7** 天。
liùbǎi měiyuán　yǒuxiàoqī shì qī tiān

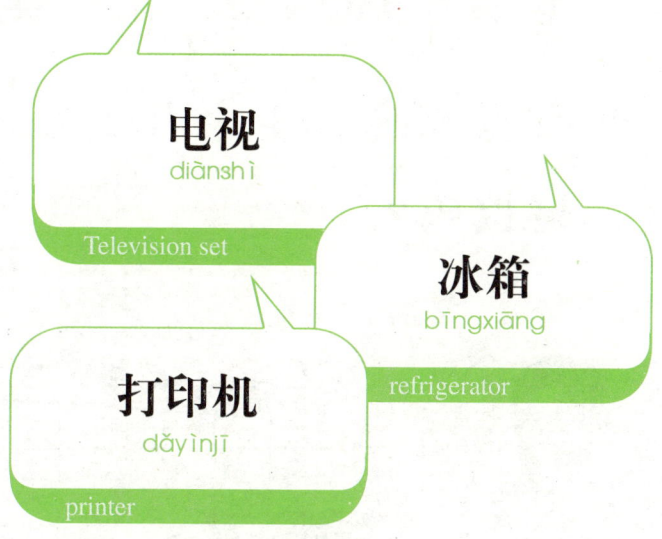

电视
diànshì

Television set

冰箱
bīngxiāng

refrigerator

打印机
dǎyìnjī

printer

NOTES

　　Prices in international markets change because of the supply-demand relations and change of exchange rates. Therefore, the sellers' quotation has a time limit, and prices might vary if it is no longer within the validity period.

93

下个月10号交货怎么样?

Xià gè yuè shí hào jiāo huò zěnmeyàng?

How about making the delivery on the tenth of next month?

● 下个月 10 号交货怎么样?
　Xià gè yuè shí hào jiāo huò zěnmeyàng?

● 有点儿晚，下个月 1 号
　Yǒudiǎnr wǎn, xià gè yuè yī hào

可以吗？
kěyǐ ma?

● How about making the delivery on the tenth of next month?
● It's somewhat late. How about the first of next month?

下个月 10 号＿＿＿＿＿＿怎么样？
xià gè yuè shí hào　　　　　zěnmeyàng

完成生产
wánchéng shēngchǎn

finish production

运到仓库
yùn dào cāngkù

deliver to the warehouse

打款
dǎ kuǎn

send the money in

NOTES

Deciding delivery time is an important content in foreign trade negotiations because commodities could be seasonal. If the delivery time is too tight, the manufacturer will face too much stress; if the delivery time is delayed, then the commodity will not make their appearance in the market on time. And as a result, the profit will be affected.

94

我们只接受信用证的付款方式。

Wǒmen zhǐ jiēshòu xìnyòngzhèng de fùkuǎn fāngshì.

We take only a letter of credit payment.

● **你们接受什么付款方式？**
Nǐmen jiēshòu shénme fùkuǎn fāngshì?

● **我们只接受信用证的付款**
Wǒmen zhǐ jiēshòu xìnyòngzhèng de fùkuǎn

方式。
fāngshì.

信用证
Letter of Credit

● What do you accept for a payment?
● We take only a letter of credit payment.

我们只接受＿＿＿＿＿＿＿＿的
wǒmen zhǐ jiēshòu   de
付款方式。
fùkuǎn fāngshì

承兑交单
chéngduìjiāodān

acceptance of bill

银行汇款
yínháng huìkuǎn

bank remittance

托收
tuōshōu

entrusted collection

NOTES

Compared to telegraphic money order and other payments, a letter of credit is the most secure payment in international trade. It can protect the interests of the buyer and seller to a maximum extent. However, the payment procedures of a letter of credit are more complicated. It is good for trade in big volumes.

95

我们收到货就马上付款。

Wǒmen shōudào huò jiù mǎshàng fùkuǎn.

We will make the payment once we get the delivery.

● 你们什么时候付款？
　Nǐmen shénme shíhou fùkuǎn?

● 我们收到货就马上付款。
　Wǒmen shōudào huò jiù mǎshàng fùkuǎn.

● When are you going to make the payment?
● We will make the payment once we get the delivery.

我们收到＿＿就马上付款。
wǒmen shōudāo　　jiù mǎshàng fùkuǎn

信用证
xìnyǒngzhěng

letter of credit

提单副本
tídān　fùběn

order copy

货物发出通知单
huòwù fāchū tōngzhīdān

delivery notification

Though Cash On Delivery is not a secure payment in international trade, yet it is simple and convenient. Cash On Delivery will be adopted when both sides are trading in relatively small amounts or when both have been long acquainted in business exchange.

96

你们的价格再优惠一些怎么样?

Nǐmen de jiàgé zài yōuhuì yìxiē zěnmeyàng?

Can your price be more preferential?

● 你们的价格再优惠一些怎么样?

Nǐmen de jiàgé zài yōuhuì yìxiē zěnmeyàng?

● 如果订购的数量多,我们可以

Rúguǒ dìnggòu de shùliàng duō, wǒmen kěyǐ

再优惠一些。

zài yōuhuì yìxiē.

● Can your price be more preferential?

● We might if your order is big enough.

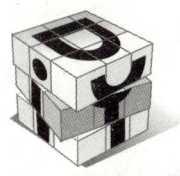

你们的价格再＿＿＿＿＿一些
nǐmen de jiàgé zài　　　　　yìxiē

怎么样？
zěnmeyàng

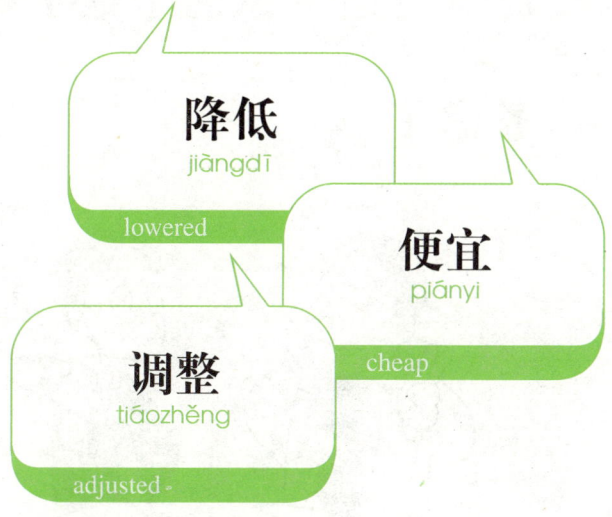

降低
jiàngdī

lowered

便宜
piányi

cheap

调整
tiáozhěng

adjusted

Price is usually the focus for both parties in trade negotiations. The buyers will asked the sellers to lower the price according to the quantity of the commodities, purchasing amount, market momentum, quotation from other competitors in the same category and other elements.

97

货物的运费你们考虑了吗？

Huòwù de yùnfèi nǐmen kǎolǜ le ma?

Have you taken into account the carriage of the goods?

● 货物的运费你们考虑了吗？

Huòwù de yùnfèi nǐmen kǎolǜ le ma?

● 考虑了。

Kǎolǜ le.

● Have you taken into account the carriage of the goods?
● Yes, we have.

货物的＿＿＿你们考虑了吗？
huòwù de　　　　　　nǐmen　kǎolǜ　le　ma

安全
ānquán

security

包装
bāozhuāng

packing

保质期
bǎozhìqī

period of quality warranty

NOTES

When the sellers are making a quotation, they must consider their production cost. In addition, they must also take the cost of carriage into account.

98

各项条款都没有问题，我们明天就签合同吧。

Gèxiàng tiáokuǎn dōu méiyǒu wèntí, wǒmen míngtiān jiù qiān hétong ba.

None of these articles have any problems. Let's sign the contract tomorrow.

● 合同审完了吗？
   Hétong shěn wánle ma?

● 审完了。各项条款都没有
   Shěn wánle.　　 Gèxiàng tiáokuǎn dōu méiyǒu

   问题，我们明天就签合同吧。
   wèntí,　　　 wǒmen míngtiān jiù qiān hétong ba.

● Have you finished checking the contract?
● Yes, we have. None of these articles have any problems.
   Let's sign the contract tomorrow.

各项 条款 都 没 有 问题，我们
gè xiàng tiáokuǎn dōu méiyǒu wèntí wǒmen

明天就签＿＿＿＿＿吧。
míngtiān jiù qiān ba

协议
xiéyì

agreement

备忘录
bèiwànglù

memory of understanding

附加协议
fùjiā xiéyì

subjoined agreement

NOTES

The buyer and seller will first draft a contract when they finish their negotiation on relevant articles. They will not sign on the official contract copy until they have scrutinized all the articles. The official contract has a legal effect once it is signed. If one party violates any article in the contract, then the other party is entitled to apply for arbitration or resort to a court, according to the breach clause.

99

关税每年都在降低。
Guānshuì měinián dōu zài jiàngdī.

Custom tariffs are decreasing year by year.

🟢 关税每年都在降低。
Guānshuì měinián dōu zài jiàngdī.

⚫ 不过，贸易壁垒越来越高。
Búguò, màoyì bìlěi yuè lái yuè gāo.

🟢 Custom tariffs are decreasing year by year.

⚫ However, trade tariffs are getting higher and higher.

_____的关税每年都在降低。
de guānshuì měinián dōu zài jiàngdī

电子产品
diànzǐ chǎnpǐn

electronic products

进口汽车
jìnkǒu qìchē

imported automobiles

纸制品
zhǐzhìpǐn

paper-made products

A custom tariff is a tax collected by a country's custom authority on the import/export commodities going through the country's borders. The payer is the import/export enterprise. There are two objectives for collecting such a tax: revenue and protection.

100

谈判是解决贸易纠纷的好办法。

Tánpàn shì jiějué màoyì jiūfēn de hǎo bànfǎ.

Negotiation is a good way to settle trade disputes.

● 谈判是解决贸易纠纷的好
Tánpàn shì jiějué màoyì jiūfēn de hǎo

办法。
bànfǎ.

● 对，我们的目标是双赢。
Duì, wǒmen de mùbiāo shì shuāngyíng.

谈判

贸易纠纷

● Negotiation is a good way to settle trade disputes.
● That's right. A win-win scenario is our goal.

_____是解决贸易纠纷
shì jiějué màoyì jiūfēn
的好办法。
de hǎo bànfǎ

协商
xiéshāng

consultation

申请仲裁
shēnqǐng zhòngcái

applying for arbitrary

调解
tiáojiě

intermediation

China is the 143rd member state joining the World Trade Organization. After its entry to WTO, when China has trade disputes with other countries, it will be able to settle those disputes through the WTO trade dispute settlement mechanism. This is done in a comparatively just and reasonable way, so as to safeguard the interests of the country and Chinese enterprises.

International Trade ⊙ 国际贸易

中国的主要商业银行
Major Commercial Banks in China

1. **中国银行**
   Zhōngguó Yínháng
   BANK OF CHINA

2. **中国工商银行**
   Zhōngguó Gōngshāng Yínháng
   INDUSTRIAL AND COMMERCIAL BANK OF CHINA

3. **中国建设银行**
   Zhōngguó Jiànshè Yínháng
   CHINA CONSTRUCTION BANK

4. **中国农业银行**
   Zhōngguó Nóngyè Yínháng
   AGRICULTURAL BANK OF CHINA

5. **交通银行**
   Jiāotōng Yínháng
   BANK OF COMMUNICATIONS

6. **中信实业银行**
   Zhōngxìn Shíyè Yínháng
   CITIC INDUSTRIAL BANK

7. **深圳发展银行**
   Shēnzhèn Fāzhǎn Yínháng
   SHENZHEN DEVELOPMENT BANK CO., LTD.

8. 广东发展银行
Guǎngdōng Fāzhǎn Yínháng
GUANGDONG DEVELOPMENT BANK

9. 中国民生银行
Zhōngguó Mínshēng Yínháng
CHINA MINSHENG BANKING CORP., LTD.

10. 招商银行
Zhāoshāng Yínháng
CHINA MERCHANTS BANK

11. 华夏银行
Huáxià Yínháng
HUAXIA BANK

12. 中国光大银行
Zhōngguó Guāngdà Yínháng
CHINA EVERBRIGHT BANK

13. 兴业银行
Xīngyè Yínháng
INDUSTRIAL BANK CO., LTD.

14. 上海浦东发展银行
Shànghǎi Pǔdōng Fāzhǎn Yínháng
SHANGHAI PUDONG DEVELOPMENT
BANK

中国常用机构网址
Commonly used websites of organizations in China

1. **中国政府网**
   Zhōngguó Zhèngfǔ Wǎng
   http://www.gov.cn

2. **中华人民共和国商务部**
   Zhōnghuá Rénmín Gònghéguó Shāngwù Bù
   http://www. mofcom.gov.cn

3. **中华人民共和国财政部**
   Zhōnghuá Rénmín Gònghéguó Cáizhèng Bù
   http://www.mof.gov.cn

4. **中华人民共和国国家工商行政管理总局**
   Zhōnghuá Rénmín Gònghéguó Guójiā Gōngshāng Xíngzhèng
   Guǎnlǐ Zǒngjú
   http://www.saic.gov.cn

5. **中华人民共和国海关总署**
   Zhōnghuá Rénmín Gònghéguó Hǎiguān Zǒngshǔ
   http://www.customs.gov.cn

6. **中华人民共和国国家税务总局**
   Zhōnghuá Rénmín Gònghéguó Guójiā Shuìwù Zǒngjú
   http://www.chinatax.gov.cn

7. **中华人民共和国国家统计局**
   Zhōnghuá Rénmín Gònghéguó Guójiā Tǒngjì Jú
   http://www.stats.gov.cn

8. 中华人民共和国国家质量监督检验检疫
   总局
   Zhōnghuá Rénmín Gònghéguó Guójiā Zhìliàng Jiāndū Jiǎnyàn
   Jiǎnyì Zǒngjú
   http://www.aqsiq.gov.cn

9. 中华人民共和国国家知识产权局
   Zhōnghuá Rénmín Gònghéguó Guójiā Zhīshi Chǎnquán Jú
   http://www.sipo.gov.cn

10. 中华人民共和国国家环境保护总局
    Zhōnghuá Rénmín Gònghéguó Guójiā Huánjìng Bǎohù Zǒngjú
    http://www.zhb.gov.cn

郑 重 声 明

高等教育出版社依法对本书享有专有出版权。任何未经许可的复制、销售行为均违反《中华人民共和国著作权法》，其行为人将承担相应的民事责任和行政责任，构成犯罪的，将被依法追究刑事责任。为了维护市场秩序，保护读者的合法权益，避免读者误用盗版书造成不良后果，我社将配合行政执法部门和司法机关对违法犯罪的单位和个人给予严厉打击。社会各界人士如发现上述侵权行为，希望及时举报，本社将奖励举报有功人员。

反盗版举报电话：(010) 58581897/58581896/58581879

传　　真：(010) 82086060

E－mail：dd@hep.com.cn

通信地址：北京市西城区德外大街 4 号
　　　　　　高等教育出版社打击盗版办公室

邮　　编：100120

购书请拨打电话：(010)58581118

图书在版编目（CIP）数据

体验汉语100句. 商务类：英语版／张红编. —北京：
高等教育出版社,2007.1(2009 重印)

ISBN 978－7－04－020521－3

Ⅰ.体⋯　Ⅱ.张⋯　Ⅲ.汉语－口语－对外汉语教学－自
学参考资料　Ⅳ.H195.4

中国版本图书馆 CIP 数据核字（2007）第 000084 号

出版发行	高等教育出版社		购书热线	010－58581118	
社　　址	北京市西城区德外大街4号		免费咨询	800－810－0598	
邮政编码	100120		网　　址	http://www.hep.edu.cn	
总　　机	010－58581000			http://www.hep.com.cn	
			网上订购	http://www.landraco.com	
				http://www.landraco.com.cn	
经　　销	蓝色畅想图书发行有限公司		畅想教育	http://www.widedu.com	
印　　刷	高等教育出版社印刷厂				
开　　本	889×1194　1/32				
印　　张	6.75		版　　次	2007 年 1 月第 1 版	
字　　数	160 000		印　　次	2009 年 4 月第 3 次印刷	

如有印装等质量问题,请到所购图书销售部门调换。　ISBN 978－7－04－020521－3